The **New** National Curriculum

D1628657

Digital Literacy for Primary Teachers

CRITICAL
TEACHING

Digital Literacy for Primary Teachers

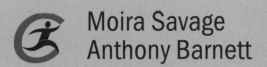

Moira Savage
Anthony Barnett

CRITICAL TEACHING

First published in 2015 by Critical Publishing Ltd

British Library Cataloguing in Publication Data
A CIP record for this book is available from the British Library

ISBN: 978-1-909682-61-0

This book is also available in the following e-book formats:

MOBI: 978-1-909682-62-7
EPUB: 978-1-909682-63-4
Adobe e-book reader: 978-1-909682-64-1

Cover and text design by Greensplash Limited
Project Management by Out of House Publishing
Typeset by Newgen Knowledge Works
Printed and bound in Great Britain by Bell & Bain, Glasgow

Critical Publishing
152 Chester Road
Northwich
CW8 4AL
www.criticalpublishing.com

Contents

Meet the authors   vi

Introduction   1

1   Defining digital literacy   6

2   Implications for teaching: digital teaching   24

3   Implications for learning: digital learning   40

4   Information literacy for teachers and learners   54

5   Creating content   69

6   Collaboration, communication and networking   89

7   Digital citizenship   105

8   Digital identity and footprints for teachers   119

9   E-safety and digital safeguarding   133

10   Conclusion   149

Index   158

Meet the authors

Moira Savage

In 1994 I entered the education profession as a primary school teacher and developed a specialism in information and communication technology (ICT) for learning and teaching. I became increasingly involved in ICT staff development culminating in joining the University of Worcester in 2003 as a senior lecturer in initial teacher training. I deliver computing/ICT modules to both undergraduate and postgraduate trainee teachers. I am also the Institute of Education e-learning coordinator and in 2011 I was awarded a University of Worcester Learning and Teaching Fellowship. My passion is exploring how new technologies can enhance learning. I have been involved in a large number of research projects and regularly supervise undergraduate and postgraduate students carrying out research.

Anthony Barnett

I moved into higher education from teaching in inner London and Kent, where most of my early experience was with primary Key Stage 2 though also included some secondary teaching and educational research. Before starting my current post at the University of Worcester in 2000 I was a science and ICT co-ordinator. My PhD is in the area of innovative research methodology. My specific interests in ICT include the role of asynchronous discussion within blended learning approaches to teaching. I'm currently also researching children's involvement in a nursery school setting using Quick Time Virtual Reality and video data collection methods. My current teaching role includes undergraduate and postgraduate design and technology, creativity in foundation subject teaching, educational studies modules focusing on issues in ICT and support for postgraduate specialist ICT students and MA students in a range of subjects.

Introduction

Overview of chapters

Digital literacy is becoming an increasingly prevalent term and this book gives a comprehensive and practical overview of what this means for today's teachers and learners. Each chapter explores key terminology, highlights links to the current Teachers' Standards and the national curriculum (summary tables are included in the conclusion). Whatever your current level of technological capability, this book equips you with the necessary understanding of the key issues, suggests areas for professional reflection and highlights ideas for further reading. Whilst new technologies are, by their nature, exciting, the book remains grounded in established principles of good learning and teaching. Successful methods are not abandoned but re-envisaged through digital technologies and services. All decisions to use technology in teaching and learning must be pedagogically driven.

Chapter 1 Defining digital literacy

The book begins by establishing a definition for digital literacy relevant to you as a primary trainee teacher. Key questions are considered; for example whether we are talking about digital literacy or literacies. Your and the children's role as consumer and author of digital content is explored. Four popular models of digital literacy are analysed and compared in relation to the computing curriculum for Key Stages 1 and 2.

Chapter 2 Implications for teaching: digital teaching

The chapter reviews established pedagogical principles and considers the role digital technologies play in assisting teachers, in the varied aspects of their role from communicating subject knowledge, assessment, feedback, administration and extending learning beyond the classroom and school day. A comprehensive consideration of technology affordances and pedagogy models is undertaken. Critical questions and case studies will help you develop confidence in your own e-learning pedagogy. Topical discussion themes are explored, for example the view of learners as digital natives and educators as digital immigrants.

Chapter 3 Implications for learning: digital learning

Chapter 3 explores the facets of digital literacy from the primary learner perspective, revisiting and building on established theories of learning linked to memory and motivation. An overview of the latest research on technology and engagement is given, for example, multimodal learning and links to memory. Further, the importance of authentic learning experiences is emphasised where learners have a sense of autonomy and ownership.

Digital technologies can offer varied opportunities for personalised learning across the curriculum and can be viewed as scaffolding tools from the constructivist perspective. You will also be challenged to consider whether, and to what extent, you can harness children's enthusiasm for gaming.

Chapter 4 Information literacy for teachers and learners

Information literacy is one of the topics that people typically think of when discussing digital literacy and indeed it is directly addressed in most models of digital literacy. Chapter 4 focuses on the dimensions of information literacy you will need professionally as a teacher and what you will need to teach children.

Information is taken to mean any representation of data including but not limited to: text, graphics, audio and video. Tools and strategies for efficiently locating materials will be discussed; for example, advanced search techniques and sources of online repositories. Approaches for critically evaluating information and sources will be discussed, including identifying the author and particular points of view being conveyed to help the learner consider quality and credibility.

Chapter 5 Creating content

Creativity might not have been the first element that sprung to mind when you started thinking about digital literacy. Through the analysis in this chapter you can see that creativity is actually a big part of digital literacy. You may need to expand your existing perspective on what creativity means now that we are focusing upon the digital realm.

Payton and Hague (2010) detail creativity as a component of digital literacy: '*the ability to think creatively and imaginatively, and to use technology to create outputs and represent knowledge in different formats and modes*' (p 10).

Belshaw expands that the creative element is about '*doing new things in new ways. It is about using technologies to perform tasks and achieve things that were previously either impossible or out-of-reach of the average person*' (2011, p 212). Hobbs suggests individuals can '*create content in a variety of forms, making use of language, images, sound, and new digital tools and technologies*' (2010).

Chapter 5 begins with exploring definitions of creativity and how these translate when we are working with digital content in cross-curricular contexts. A range of learning tasks will be identified and options for creating content using a variety of digital tools, off and online, will be discussed. Classrooms vary greatly in terms of what technology is available day-to-day for learners to utilise, and some of the popular items will be identified alongside some simple deployment suggestions (iPads, cameras, voice recorders, etc).

Chapter 6 Collaboration, communication and networking

The affordances of a networked world include new possibilities for collaboration and communication. The Key Stage 2 computing programmes of study requires that pupils are taught to '*understand computer networks including the internet; how they can provide multiple services, such as the world wide web; and the opportunities they offer for communication and collaboration*' (DfE, 2013).

Hobbs discusses people '*working individually and collaboratively to share knowledge and solve problems*' (2010). In an educational context Payton and Hague (2010) discuss children's digital literacy capability as including:

> the ability to work successfully with others to collaboratively create and share meaning and understanding. To develop the skills of team-work, to be able to work together when using technology and to understand how technology can support collaboration both inside the classroom and in the wider world.
>
> (Payton and Hague, 2010, p 10)

Chapter 6 covers these dimensions, giving an overview of common Web 2.0 tools including: blogs, wikis, podcasting and virtual worlds. Understanding the functionality of tools, advantages, disadvantages and risks, will enable you to match the tool to the appropriate learning and teaching opportunity. Examples are given of both teachers and learners using these tools in different curriculum contexts. Web-based publishing (eg blogs) can provide learners with opportunities to write for a real audience and add meaning to their work.

Chapter 7 Digital citizenship

If you were to ask the average teenager whether they had ever downloaded a game, music track or video without paying for it you might be surprised by their response. Alongside the wealth of exciting opportunities of being digitally literate you need a professional awareness of digital citizenship and what this entails; for example, an understanding of digital rights and responsibilities.

Digital artefacts, and who has ownership and rights to use them, are a confusing area. You are given some straightforward advice on using and repurposing existing web-based materials and directed to external sources of advice and materials; for example Creative Commons licences. Belshaw highlighted that '*creating something new*' can now involve '*using and remixing content from other sources*' (2011, pp 208–9). '*Therefore understanding how and for what purposes content can be appropriated, reused and remixed*' is one important element of digital literacy (Belshaw, 2011, p 209).

Generic principles of data security will be discussed and reference made to external sources of advice alongside guidance on what questions to ask in relation to local protocols in place (or not) within educational establishments.

Chapter 8 Digital identity and footprints for teachers

The JISC definition of digital literacy contains a direct reference to '*career and identity management*', emphasising the need for individuals to manage '*their digital reputation and online identity*' (2014). Chapter 8 is dedicated to ensuring you are fully aware of how your personal online activities and your digital footprint need to convey your professionalism in line with the Teachers' Standards:

> *A teacher is expected to demonstrate consistently high standards of personal and professional conduct ... Uphold public trust in the profession and maintain high standards of ethics and behaviour.*
>
> (DfE, 2013)

This chapter identifies key school policy documents and their indicative content that you must be aware of including, for example, an Acceptable Use Policy. A detailed exploration of what your digital footprint typically consists of, how to limit past elements you may not want to be public and how to build a positive online profile, is contained. Common-sense guidance on protocols for using school and personal equipment for teaching and learning is given to ensure both that your privacy is maintained and safeguarding measures to protect children are adhered to. Unfortunately it is a reality that some teachers become victims of cyberbullying from prior or current pupils or parents. The chapter gives practical advice on how to deal with such situations and sources of support. Hopefully following the suggestions in the chapter for managing your online identity will help prevent this ever happening to you.

Chapter 9 E-safety and digital safeguarding

Payton and Hague's (2010) model of digital literacy was written with school-aged children in mind and directly addresses the crucial area of e-safety:

> *The ability to stay safe when using digital technologies, such as the internet and mobile phones, and to understand what constitutes appropriate use and appropriate content.*
>
> (2010, p 6)

It is not absent in the other models but less directly addressed from a teaching standpoint; for example, in Belshaw's model these themes would emerge under the *civic* element.

The computing programmes of study at both Key Stage 1 and 2 directly highlight e-safety although the term is not directly used. At Key Stage 1 pupils should be taught to: '*use technology safely and respectfully, keeping personal information private; know where to go for help and support when they have concerns about material on the internet*' (DfE, 2013, p 189). Further at Key Stage 2 pupils should be taught to: '*use technology safely, respectfully and responsibly; know a range of ways to report concerns and inappropriate behaviour*' (DfE, 2013, p 189).

A significant amount of time in the chapter is devoted to identifying and understanding risk and potential dangers. Particular themes explored from a child's perspective are sexual risks, cyberbullying and commercial risks. Tried and tested resources are suggested to assist you in understanding and teaching this essential element of digital literacy. A research-informed overview of children's use of technologies is given, encompassing social networking, instant messaging and gaming, for example. You may be anxious about how to respond should a child make a disclosure and some simple guidance is given here and pointers to ensure you obtain the protocol information you need from your particular setting.

Chapter 10 Conclusion

The concluding chapter offers a brief review of the book and the key issues that have been explored from a primary teacher's perspective. The book finishes by predicting several trends which are likely to grow in prominence over the next few years in primary technology enhanced learning and teaching. Several one-to-one iPad projects are listed for you to explore. The remainder of the chapter offers suggestions for on-going personal and professional development including key organisations, annual events and courses.

References

Belshaw, D (2011) *What is 'Digital Literacy'?* [online] Available at: neverendingthesis.com/doug-belshaw-edd-thesis-final.pdf (accessed 31 October 2014).

Department for Education (2013) *The National Curriculum in England: Framework Document.* [online] Available at: www.gov.uk/government/uploads/system/uploads/attachment_data/file/239033/PRIMARY_national_curriculum_-_Computing.pdf (accessed 31 October 2014).

Hobbs, R (2010) *Digital and Media Literacy: A Plan of Action.* [online] Available at: www.knight-comm.org/wpcontent/uploads/2010/12/Digital_and_Media_Literacy_A_Plan_of_Action.pdf (accessed 8 August 2014).

Joint Information Systems Committee (2014) *Developing Digital Literacies.* [online] Available at: www.jiscinfonet.ac.uk/whole-infokit/?infokit=11013 (accessed 31 October 2014).

Payton, S and Hague, C (2010) *Digital Literacy in Practice: Case Studies of Primary and Secondary Classrooms.* Futurelab. [online] Available at: www2.futurelab.org.uk/resources/documents/project_reports/digital_literacy_case_studies.pdf (accessed 31 October 2014).

1 Defining digital literacy

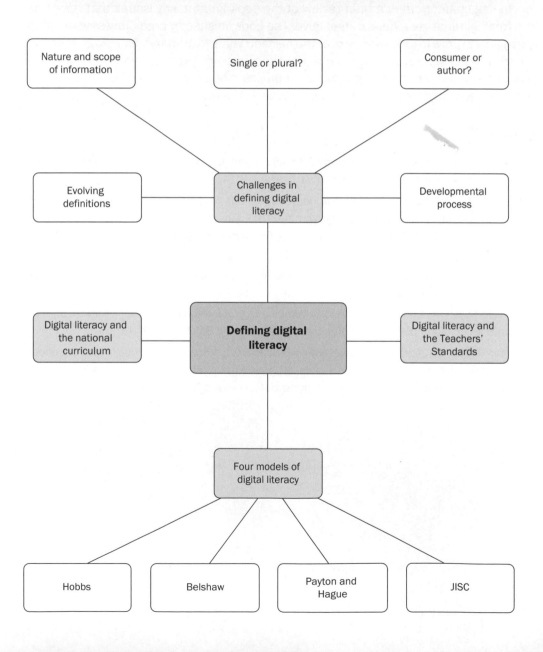

Introduction

Has the nature of literacy changed now that a great deal of information and content is digitised? Facer (2009) reminds us that '*learners will continue to need to learn the principles of reading and writing print and writing will always be a significant form of communication with high cultural value*' (p 101). However, representing and communicating meaning in today's primary classrooms is increasingly mediated by technology. Both the learner and the teacher can opt to use digitally enhanced combinations of visual, audio and text modalities. Therefore, the '*process of writing will inevitably change with technological developments that will facilitate extensive on-screen writing*' (Facer, 2009, p 101). That screen comes in many different sizes and shapes including PCs, laptops, tablets, smartphones, phablets, cameras, iPods, etc. The formats include SMS, instant messages, status updates, blogs, wikis, games, websites, programs, microblogging (eg tweets), music, podcasts, photos, graphics, videos, webinars, animations, vlogs (videologs), mashups, etc. Text can be augmented with auditory, static and dynamic visuals, interactive and non-linear content. As an educator you should resist disregarding these new approaches and instead embrace them, *in addition to* traditional forms, accompanied with an understanding of impact, time, place, purpose and audience.

> *The range of multimodal texts and technologies in use are likely to lead to modes other than writing becoming persuasive when undertaking daily activities. Likewise, repertoires of literacy practice will continue to expand and diversify across different technologies, creating a complex environment and challenging the dominance of writing.*
>
> (Facer, 2009, p 101)

Challenges in defining digital literacy

Many of you will already have an understanding of the term literacy and what it means to be literate. In the traditional interpretation it means to be able to read and write. This definition largely reflects the time in which it came in to common use and the dominant tools for accessing and communicating knowledge and understanding beyond verbal discourse, ie written and printed text in physical forms. One simple way to extend this traditional definition would be to say it is about '*reading media and writing (producing) media*' (Ryberg and Georgsen, 2010, p 91). An understanding of digital literacy can be developed from these earlier definitions; after all it is still about accessing, interpreting, understanding and communication of information, knowledge and understanding. However, now digital technologies mean that there is greater choice in the mode and platform of that interaction (with) and communication (of) information in all its possible forms. Throughout this book the term *information* is taken as meaning any symbolic representation of meaning in any form; including numbers, text, visual artefacts and sound.

This chapter suggests that digital literacy is far more than a list of technical competencies in which to train both teachers and children. A competency-only perspective is limiting, as it does not fully appreciate the potential impact on learners: for example, empowering creative forms of expression and access to decentralised information in multiple formats. Several key questions to be explored include:

- should we be discussing digital literacy or literacies?
- does digital literacy evolve alongside technology?
- are certain values and attitudes implied?
- are we consumers or producers of digital content?

Critical questions

To help you understand your starting point, take a few moments to reflect upon your thoughts about the rise of technology in society and education. Spend some time examining what beliefs and values underpin those opinions.

» *Are they based on fact, popular opinion or research?*

» *Are there any emotional responses involved; for example, fear of technology or fear that children you will be teaching may have a greater capability level?*

When you have finished reading this book you may want to reflect back on your initial responses.

The nature and scope of information

Critical questions

» *What forms of information do primary-aged children typically have access to?*

» *How and where have they accessed that information?*

» *What level of teacher input/guidance has there been?*

It is important for you as a teacher to consider how children's access to information has changed over time. In pre-internet schooldays access to information was often limited to a range of books with printed text and pictures which had been preselected (filtered) by teachers or parents, occasionally augmented by a weekly live television programme or visit to the local library. Generally the information range was comparatively narrow and pre-filtered. It wasn't always portable and generally didn't allow for revisiting or remixing.

Critical question

» *To what extent do you agree/disagree with the following statements by Facer about literacy?*

'... some argue that the use of technology might result in losses of traditional (literacy) skills. Others claim that traditional literacy skills (reading and synthesising) are more central than ever in engaging with complex and huge amounts of data' *(Facer, 2009, p 100).*

Single or plural?

Critical question

» *Try writing your own definition for digital literacy. On what grounds have you included or excluded items?*

The term digital literacy itself is the subject of much discussion and generally the term is broken down into several sub-components and many will use the term digital literacies to emphasise this plurality. Did you find your list impossible to fit into one neat statement? Throughout this book when the term digital literacy is used it is intended that you acknowledge this plurality and interpret the term as meaning digital literacies.

Consumer or author?

When talking about digital literacy it is easy to dwell on children and adults as consumers; for example, carrying out research online on a topic for a school project; extracting text and searching for pictures to add, etc. Whilst this information accessing, retrieval and processing is an important component, digital literacy goes far beyond these acts as you will see throughout this book. One important mindset to explore is that to be digitally literate means being both a consumer and an author (producer) of digital content and having the skills, knowledge, understanding, values and attitudes embodied within both roles.

Resnick (2012a) was very much influenced by Papert's view that children should go beyond being consumers and be able to '*design, create and express themselves with new technologies*'. Resnick (2013), when talking about the online Scratch community (a visual educational programming language for children), details how children '*begin to see themselves as creators and designers, as people who can make things with digital media, not just browse, chat and play games*'. Chapter 5 explores creating content in detail and suggest classroom-appropriate forms this may take.

Evolving definitions

The Joint Information Systems Committee (JISC) describes *digital literacies* as '*those capabilities which fit an individual for living, learning and working in a digital society*' (2014). This theme is echoed in the computing national curriculum statement:

> *Computing also ensures that pupils become digitally literate – able to use, and express themselves and develop their ideas through, information and communication technology – at a level suitable for the future workplace and as active participants in a digital world.*
>
> (DfE, 2013)

The term future is important here: one certainty about technology is change and many would argue that an absolute fixed definition is not possible as the tools and mechanisms constantly evolve. JISC (2014) articulate this need for a fluid conceptualisation:

What it means to be digitally literate changes over time and across contexts, so digital literacies are essentially a set of academic or professional situated practices supported by diverse and changing technologies.

Given this uncertainty, one useful way for you to navigate the complexity is to focus upon the cognitive process or purpose underlying the action/activities and acknowledge that precise forms will vary and evolve. We would suggest there is a self-limiting danger in you trying to see digital literacy as gaining competency in a particular application or online service.

Developmental process

It is useful for you to think about digital literacy as a continuum. You will be on a journey and in the modern world there is not a point where absolute mastery is attained. JISC (2014) make reference to Beetham and Sharpe's 2010 work, which suggests a *'process where individuals become increasingly proficient eventually reaching a level of fluency'*. Therefore, *'digital literacy can be considered a developmental process from access and functional skills to higher-level capabilities and identities'*.

Belshaw (2011) agrees that *'digital literacy is a condition, not a threshold and, as with all conditions requires maintenance and context'* (p 214). Although specific references to digital literacy are made in the computing curriculum we would encourage you to consider it in a cross-curricular sense, activities need to be authentic and have purpose for children.

Four models of digital literacy

The following four popular models of digital literacy explored in this section will assist you in gaining a rounded understanding of what is meant by digital literacy:

- Hobbs (2010);

- Belshaw (2011);

- Payton and Hague (2010) for Futurelab;

- Joint Information Systems Committee (JISC) (2014).

You will notice that despite differences in terminology there is considerable overlap in the models.

Hobbs' model

The Hobbs (2010) model defines *'digital and media literacy as a constellation of life skills that are necessary for full participation in our media-saturated, information-rich society'*. These include the ability to do the following:

- *Make responsible choices and access information by locating and sharing materials and comprehending information and ideas*

- *Analyse messages in a variety of forms by identifying the author, purpose and point of view, and evaluating the quality and credibility of the content*

- *Create content in a variety of forms, making use of language, images, sound, and new digital tools and technologies*

- *Reflect on one's own conduct and communication behaviour by applying social responsibility and ethical principles*

- *Take social action by working individually and collaboratively to share knowledge and solve problems in the family, workplace and community, and by participating as a member of a community.*

(pp vii–viii)

Critical questions

» *In the Hobbs model can you identify the cognitive processes (eg comprehension) involved and arrange these in a hierarchy similar to the traditional Bloom's taxonomy model? (See en.wikipedia.org/wiki/Bloom's_taxonomy if you are not already familiar with this model from your professional studies.)*

» *What values and attitudes can you identify embedded within this definition?*

» *How does this contrast with your definition of digital literacy that you wrote at the beginning of this chapter?*

JISC model

JISC (2014) (see Figure 1.1 overleaf) states that *'digital literacy looks beyond functional IT skills to describe a richer set of digital behaviours, practices and identities'*. There are significant areas of overlap with the Hobbs model.

For example:

- *information literacy: find, interpret, evaluate, manage and share information*
(JISC, 2014)

echoes Hobbs:

- *Access: finding and using media and technology tools skilfully and sharing appropriate and relevant information with others* (2010, p 19).

Belshaw's model

Another popular model is by Belshaw (2011) in which he details eight components of digital literacy:

1. *Cultural*: digital literacy is seen as contextual and situational with co-constructed norms of conduct.

    In each of these contexts are found different codes and ways of operating, things that are accepted or encouraged as well as those that are frowned upon and rejected.

(2011, p 207)

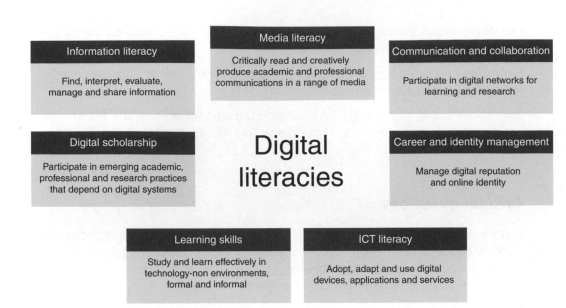

Figure 1.1 *Seven elements model of digital literacies*
Source: JISC (2014).

Examples would include the use of capitals to suggest shouting in SMS messages, informal language and terminology in a gaming forum compared to the choices of language and phrasing which might be used in a class topic wiki to be shared with parents. Rather than jumping to criticise children as being impolite or unable to speak standard English, etc, we would suggest understanding the complex nuances that young learners are applying in understanding the impact on the audience and making sophisticated choices in terminology and phrasing in these different situations. All individuals are prone to adopting characteristics of a sub-culture to gain a sense of belonging and this reflects a deep understanding of context. As a teacher part of your role is to help children explore the rich variety of communication and what is appropriate for different contexts. Texting in abbreviations does not mean inability to spell, despite opinions in the popular media, it is just an efficient form of communication alongside symbols such as emoticons within a particular genre. Belshaw sums this up nicely: '*Digital literacies are not solely about technical proficiency but about the issues, norms and habits of mind surrounding technologies used for a particular purpose*' (2011, p 207).

A pedagogical point made by Belshaw is that acquisition of digital literacy in cultural terms is best done '*through immersion in a range of digital environments*' (2011, p 207). Therefore, you should consider the range of digital environments you are providing opportunities for children to explore in the classroom with an awareness of the environments they access beyond the classroom.

2. *Cognitive*: here Belshaw prompts us to think about the cognitive dimension of digital literacy beyond '*using a set of technical tools*' (eg carrying out an internet search on a search engine) and focus on the ability to '*use a set of cognitive tools*' (2011, p 208).

Exposure to various ways of conceptualising and interacting in digital spaces helps develop the cognitive element of digital literacies. It is not the practise of using tools, but rather the habits of mind such use can develop.

(2011, p 208)

This emphasis on *mind expansion* by Belshaw (2011, p 208) resonates with a statement from Resnick (2012b) explaining why the *activity of making* (being an author) *is so important in the learning process*:

When you make something in the world, it becomes an external representation of the ideas in your head. It enables you to play with your ideas and gain a better understanding of the possibilities and limitations of your ideas. Why didn't it work the way I expected? I wonder what would happen if I changed this piece of it? By giving an external form and shape to your ideas, you also provide opportunities for other people to play with your ideas and give suggestions on your ideas? Why didn't I think of that? How can I make it more useful to people?

(Resnick, 2012b, pp 50–1)

3.   *Constructive*: Belshaw explains this component as '*pertaining to creating something new, including using and remixing content from other sources to create something original*' (2011, pp 208–9). Further, '*one part of the constructive element of digital literacies is therefore understanding how and for what purposes content can be appropriated, reused and remixed*' (2011, p 209). New forms of copyright including Creative Commons licensing will be explored in Chapter 7 on digital citizenship.

4.   *Communicative*: in Belshaw's model this focuses upon '*understanding how communications media work. It is, in essence, the nuts and bolts of how to communicate in digital networked environments*' (2011, p 209). A tension here exists for teachers, '*as developing a true understanding of networks ... involves not only learning about them but being part of them*' (2011, p 210). In this respect safeguarding and e-safety issues need to be carefully navigated and strategies for doing this are suggested in Chapter 9 on e-safety. Interestingly the computing national curriculum now requires that Key Stage 2 children are taught to:

Understand computer networks including the internet; how they can provide multiple services ... and the opportunities they offer for communication and collaboration.

(DfE, 2013)

Communication and collaboration will be explored in Chapter 6.Whilst safeguarding continues to be paramount a cultural change may be needed in schools that have traditionally tended to ban outright access to online interactive communities.

5.   *Confident*: Belshaw here refers to the unique affordance of digital technologies, compared to physical world equivalents, ie the low-risk opportunity to experiment. The opportunity to try something without knowing the final outcome and the capacity to undo, redo, etc, until the desired result is achieved. This provisionality component is one of the most powerful affordances of digital technologies and pedagogically creates a freedom for children to experiment, particularly in relation to problem solving.

> *... a confidence based on the understanding that the digital environment can be more forgiving in regards to experimentation ... which ... allows individuals to approach situations in digital environments differently.*
>
> (2011, p 210)

Affordances of digital technologies will be covered in greater detail in Chapter 2.

6. *Creative*: Belshaw expands that the creative element is about '*doing new things in new ways. It is about using technologies to perform tasks and achieve things that were previously either impossible or out-of-reach of the average person*' (2011, p 212). From a pedagogical perspective this is about '*redefinition (e.g. a multimodal, collaborative webpage)*' rather than '*substitution (e.g. typing out in best activities)*' (2011, p 212). Chapter 2 will explore the SAMR (Substitution, Augmentation, Redefinition and Modification) framework for considering the nature of tasks using digital technologies (Puentedura, 2013).

7. *Critical*: in Belshaw's work this dimension involves acknowledging and questioning conventions, assumptions, power relationships, etc, and is closely linked with *civic* (2011, pp 212–13).

8. *Civic*: '*The civic element is about participation, social justice and civic responsibility*' (2011, p 212). This is echoed in the primary computing curriculum with reference to the aim that all pupils should be '*responsible users*' (DfE, 2013).

Critical question

» *Belshaw (2013) proposes that* '*digital literacies are plural, subjective and highly context dependent*'. *To what extent do you agree/disagree with this statement?*

Payton and Hague's model

This model was published by Futurelab and, unlike the societal level of the Hobbs and Belshaw models, has educational contexts as a specific focus. Several primary case studies are recommended at the end of the chapter to illustrate dimensions of this model.

Table 1.1 Components of digital literacy

(table created from extracts from Payton and Hague, 2010, p 10)

Components of digital literacy	Creativity	The ability to think creatively and imaginatively, and to use technology to create outputs and represent knowledge in different formats and modes.
	Critical thinking and evaluation	Being able to use reasoning skills to engage with digital media and its content, to question, analyse, scrutinise and evaluate it and to formulate and support arguments about it and the way it is used. Critical thinking involves being reflective, developing insight about underlying assumptions, interpreting meaning and determining significance in order to understand and make sense of the world.

Table 1.1 (cont.)

Components of digital literacy	Cultural and social understanding	The ability to recognise that there are social, cultural and historical influences that shape the creation of digital content and our understanding of it. This involves understanding how your own and others' perspectives have been informed by cultural heritages and being aware of the social and cultural contexts in which digital media is created and used.
	Collaboration	The ability to work successfully with others to collaboratively create and share meaning and understanding. To develop the skills of team-work, to be able to work together when using technology and to understand how technology can support collaboration both inside the classroom and in the wider world.
	The ability to find and select information	To define what sort of information you need for a task or activity, to know where and how to find information, to critically engage with sources to select relevant, valuable and reliable information and to be aware of intellectual property issues related to plagiarism and copyright.
	Effective communication	Being able to clearly express ideas and feelings so that others can understand them. Having an understanding of the different modes (visual, audio, textual, etc) in which meaning can be represented and showing an awareness of the needs of particular audiences. Understanding how technology can support this and how to communicate effectively using different types of technology.
	e-safety	The ability to stay safe when using digital technologies, such as the internet and mobile phones, and to understand what constitutes appropriate use and appropriate content.
	Functional skills	Knowing how to use a range of different technologies competently and having the skills and flexibility to adapt this knowledge to learn how to use new technologies.

CASE STUDY 1

Digital captain's log: key stage 2 literacy and science activity

Payton and Hague (2010, pp 17–22). The full case study and discussion can be accessed at: www2.futurelab.org.uk/resources/documents/project_reports/digital_literacy_case_studies.pdf.

Table 1.2 *Summary of digital captain's log activity (Payton and Hague, 2010, pp 17–22)*

Task given to children	**Digital captain's log** *Your mission: create a video diary to describe to your class the experience of exploring another planet. Use internet research to boost your imagination and creativity.*
Context	*Year 3 children working on a cross curricular unit of learning entitled 'space: the final frontier'.*
Teacher aims	*The overall teaching aim was to describe for their peers the fictional experience of exploring the planet using what they had learnt from the internet research to inform their imagination and creativity.* *The teacher aimed to improve children's digital literacy including:* • *internet research skills;* • *ability to assess the relevance and reliability of digital sources;* • *effective communication;* • *representing information in a visual format.*
Equipment/resources	*Digital video cameras and editing software* *Rocket launch video as a stimulus*

Critical question

» *Using the Payton and Hague model given in Table 1.1, identify those aspects of digital literacy you feel you could develop carrying out a similar activity in your own classroom.*

One strength of activities of this nature is that they require the children to search with a purpose and, most importantly, use the information they find to achieve a particular goal. We have often heard trainees and teachers complain that children simply print pages or copy and paste sections from the internet for homework tasks. Here the child is only partly to blame as the task probably did not include an application stage, ie asking the child to do or achieve something with that new information. The captain's log example also employs the useful tip of requiring that new information acquired be presented in a different media. These activities require the child to engage with the new information at a much higher level.

Digital literacy and the national curriculum

The national curriculum for computing begins with the following statement regarding the *purpose of study*:

> *Computing also ensures that pupils become digitally literate – able to use, and express themselves and develop their ideas through, information and communication technology – at a level suitable for the future workplace and as active participants in a digital world.*

(DfE, 2013)

The phrase 'active participants in a digital world' recognises the increasing value placed academically, socially and in employment of being digitally literate. Facer observed that for young people (2009):

> New purposes for literacy will continue to emerge from the ability to communicate across space and time with known and unknown people. These will be supported by developments of mobile and social networking technologies and the increasingly embedded character of these in the everyday will produce emergent and fluid sub-cultures and sharing networks which enable a broad set of practices with text. Overall, the blurring of traditional distinctions between producer (author) and consumer (reader) will escalate, and will require a complex range of skills, knowledge and understanding.
>
> (Facer, 2009, p 100)

Digital literacy is also referred to in the computing curriculum aims to ensure that all pupils:

- can evaluate and apply information technology, including new or unfamiliar technologies, analytically to solve problems;
- are responsible, competent, confident and creative users of information and communication technology.

(DfE, 2013)

Table 1.3 details the programme of study requirements from Key Stages 1 and 2 that have strong digital literacy components. The emphasis has been added by the author and you will notice many terms from the models of digital literacy that have been discussed above.

Table 1.3 Digital literacy components of the Key Stage 1 and 2 computing programmes of study (DfE, 2013)

Key Stage 1 pupils should be taught to:	Key Stage 2 pupils should be taught to:
• use technology purposefully to create, organise, store, manipulate and retrieve digital content; • recognise **common uses** of information technology **beyond school**; • use technology **safely and respectfully**, keeping personal information private; identify where to go for help and support when they have concerns about content or contact on the internet or other online technologies.	• understand **computer networks** including the internet; how they can provide multiple services, such as the world wide web; and the opportunities they offer for **communication** and **collaboration**; • use **search technologies** effectively, appreciate **how results are selected and ranked**, and be **discerning in evaluating** digital content; • **select, use** and **combine** a **variety** of software (including internet services) on a **range of digital devices** to **design and create** a range of programs, systems and **content** that accomplish given goals, including **collecting, analysing, evaluating and presenting data and information**; • use technology **safely, respectfully** and **responsibly**; recognise acceptable/unacceptable behaviour; identify a range of ways to report concerns about content and contact.

Critical question

According to Facer (2009), as a twenty-first century citizen 'it will be increasingly valuable to create multimodal texts that can operate across a range of platforms, to recognise the affordances of a mode will become a key competency, along with the choice of media, skills in use of various modes, and the ability to analyse multimodal texts, and to rapidly critique information from a range of sources' (p 100).

» *Which of the elements raised by Facer can you identify in the programmes of study?*

Viewing the national curriculum through the Hobbs (2010) model it is possible to identify where many of the domains of digital literacies have been picked up for primary children (see Table 1.4, emphasis added by the author).

Table 1.4 *Links between the Hobbs model and the computing programmes of study*

Hobbs 2010 *(pp vii–viii)*	Computing curriculum references for Key Stage 1 and Key Stage 2 (DfE, 2013)
Make responsible choices and **access** *information by* **locating** *and sharing materials and comprehending information and ideas.*	*KS2 use* **search** *technologies effectively, appreciate how results are selected and ranked, and be* **discerning** *in* **evaluating** *digital content.*
Analyse messages in a variety of forms by identifying the author, purpose and point of view, and **evaluating** *the* **quality** *and* **credibility** *of the content.*	
Create content *in a* **variety of forms**, *making use of* **language, images, sound**, *and* **new digital tools** *and technologies.*	*Key Stage 1 use technology purposefully to* **create**, *organise, store, manipulate and retrieve digital content.* *Key Stage 2* **select, use** *and* **combine a variety of software** *(including internet services) on a* **range of digital devices** *to design and* **create a range** *of programs, systems and* **content** *that accomplish given goals, including collecting, analysing, evaluating and presenting data and information.*
Reflect on one's own **conduct** *and communication* **behaviour** *by applying social responsibility and ethical principles.*	*Key Stage 1 use technology* **safely and respectfully**. *Key Stage 2 use* **technology safely, respectfully and responsibly**; *recognise acceptable/ unacceptable* **behaviour**.
Take social action by **working individually and collaboratively** *to share knowledge and solve problems in the family, workplace and community, and by participating as a* **member of a community**.	*Key Stage 1 recognise common uses of information technology beyond school.* *Key Stage 2 understand computer networks including the internet; how they can provide multiple services, such as the world wide web; and the opportunities they offer for* **communication and collaboration**.

Critical question

» *Can you identify where the eight digital literacies (cultural, cognitive, constructive, communicative, confident, creative, critical and civic) proposed by Belshaw occur in the computing curriculum? Are there any missing?*

Digital literacy and the Teachers' Standards

> *Digital literacy is an important entitlement for all young people in an increasingly digital culture ... Indeed, if formal education seeks to prepare young people to make sense of the world and to thrive socially, intellectually and economically, then it cannot afford to ignore the social and cultural practices of digital literacy that enable people to make the most of their multiple interactions with digital technology and media.*

> (Payton and Hague, 2010, p 9)

The legal entitlement for children to be taught elements of digital literacy is clearly embodied in the computing programmes of study. Beyond this there is a general agreement with Payton and Hague's statement that if we are preparing learners for their future academic and work lives then teaching digital literacy in a meaningful way in primary schools is a key stepping stone. Often one of the best ways to teach is to set an example in your own teaching behaviours in the classroom.

Despite notions of young people today being *digital natives* (Prensky, 2001) or part of the *net generation*, this is not always universally true due to a variety of factors affecting access or patterns of use (Oblinger and Oblinger, 2005, cited in Ryberg and Georgsen, 2010, p 89). Therefore, Ryberg and Georgsen pertinently remind us:

> *Whilst the ideas of young people as particularly digitally literate do have some merit, it is also becoming increasingly clear that not all young people acquire the necessary competencies or literacies through informal use of technology. Educational institutions therefore play a pivotal role in ensuring that all young people attain the necessary competencies.*

> (Ryberg and Georgsen, 2010, p 89)

As a teacher, recognising differential access, experiences and competencies is always key and likewise in relation to digital literacy. Ensure your decisions are based on formative assessment and dialogue and not assumptions that all children are digitally literate from their out-of-school experiences. As with any subject the Teachers' Standards require that you are '*aware of pupils' capabilities and their prior knowledge, and plan teaching to build on these*' (DfE, 2011, p 10).

Hopefully, the definitions explored in this chapter have persuaded you of the academic rigour and extent of digital literacy. The Teachers' Standards remind you that as a professional you are required to '*keep your knowledge and skills up-to-date and be self-critical*' (DfE, 2011, p 10).

iteracy pushes the educational boundaries for teachers. In addition to content decisions an effective teacher must have a repertoire of communication strategies. This demands that you have a good, and continually evolving, level of competency in different modes of communication and an understanding of modal (textual, visual, aural, etc) affordances. Beyond that, a truly twenty-first century teacher will have some understanding of how these modalities complement, layer and enrich each other in teaching and learning activities. Technology can be one approach in creating '*a stimulating environment for pupils*' (DfE, 2011, p 10).

Critical questions

Spend a few moments considering theories of learning you may have encountered already in your training: for example, constructivism or learning styles.

» *How does digital literacy fit within your understanding of these pedagogical approaches?*

» *Can digital tools be considered scaffolding techniques for learners?*

The Teachers' Standards require you to '*demonstrate knowledge and understanding of how pupils learn and how this impacts on teaching*' and this includes digital literacy (DfE, 2011, p 10). In the following quote from Facer (2009) she is not directly talking about teachers but makes a parallel point about the need for understanding and research about the interplay of multimodality, cognition and communication:

The choice of mode and thus modal affordances will become more important for the work of design with respect to knowledge, creativity and communication. The layers of visual symbols, audio, print and hyperlinked meaning-making pathways will highlight the need for a deeper understanding of how modal layers create meanings. Added to this the development of the skills to bring these modes into different kinds of configurations and relations will increase in value.

(Facer, 2009, p 100)

Multimodality as a topic is explored in Chapter 3.

Conclusion

Several of the definitions argue that '*digital literacies are composite and situational accomplishments, which should not be reduced to piece-meal curricular units, but taught as organic, complex engagement with different literacy practices*' (Ryberg and Georgsen, 2010, p 90). It is recommended that you don't view the digital elements of the computing curriculum as an isolated subject but as core to learning in all subjects. Therefore effective teaching will be cross-curricula and purposeful. Offering children choices in the form, frequency and audience to express their ideas is powerful motivationally. The Teachers' Standards require you to '*reflect systematically on the effectiveness of lessons and approaches to teaching*' (DfE, 2011, p 11). Not all your initial attempts teaching with technology will be an outright success but reflection will serve as a tool to ensure your digital literacy evolves with a growing understanding of its pedagogical potential.

Developing digital literacy across the curriculum is about more than motivating and engaging learners with digital technology; it is about supporting young people to make sense of the world and to take a full and active part in social, cultural, economic, civic and intellectual life both now and in the future.

(Payton and Hague, 2010, p 9)

Critical points

» *You should avoid thinking of traditional notions of literacy and digital literacy as an either/or. You should embrace both, and view digital literacy as a development of traditional notions of literacy reflecting the current context for primary-aged learners.*

» *You should think of digital literacy as representing a plurality of wide ranging elements including knowledge, skills, understanding, values and attitudes.*

» *The book seeks to expand your interpretation of digital literacy beyond being a consumer to being an author alongside the children in your classroom.*

Further reading and useful resources

There are many websites devoted to digital literacy. Here are a few to explore, you may want to bookmark ones you find particularly helpful.

For an international perspective useful generic resources on digital literacy include:

• *US Digital Literacy: America's Internet Resource for Instructional Technology*, digitalliteracy. us. Particularly useful are the digital toolkits available (accessed 31 October 2014).

• *New Zealand Inquiry into 21st Century Learning Environment and Digital Literacy: Report to Parliament 2012*, www.parliament.nz/en-nz/pb/sc/documents/reports/50DBSCH_ SCR5695_1/inquiry-into-21st-century-learning-environments-and-digital (accessed 31 October 2014).

• edtechpd.sdcoe.net/home/glossary hosts a technology glossary (accessed 31 October 2014).

Resources for teaching digital literacy in the primary computing curriculum include:

• *Computing at School & Naace, 2013. Computing in the National Curriculum: A Guide for Primary Teachers*, www.naace.co.uk/curriculum/primaryguide (accessed 31 October 2014). These reflect the current curriculum requirement for 2014.

• JISC suggest a range of UK digital literacy frameworks on this page: jiscdesignstudio.pbworks. com/w/page/46601840/DL%20conceptual%20frameworks (accessed 31 October 2014).

• The *conceptual framework for mapping common tasks and practices* is useful in terms of deciding which tool/application for particular activities. There are some great diagrammatic representations accessed via the embedded links: cmapspublic3.ihmc.us/rid=1KY550GR7-1YNJ9RF-CYP5/overview.html (accessed 31 October 2014).

• Payton and Hague (2010) provide some practical classroom examples with primary aged children in their publication: *Digital Literacy in Practice: Case Studies of Primary and*

Secondary Classrooms. A PDF version of the document can be accessed from their website at: www2.futurelab.org.uk/resources/documents/project_reports/digital_literacy_case_studies.pdf (accessed 31 October 2014). I would recommend viewing these examples from across the curriculum: *Digital Captain's Log Key Stage 02, Literacy & Science* (p 11; referred to earlier in this chapter); *Animated Stories Key Stage 02, Literacy* (p 15); *Recording, Reviewing and Evaluating Learning Key Stage 02, Science* (p 18); *Digital Prospectus Key Stage 02, Cross Curricular* (p 22).

• Another Payton and Hague publication for Futurelab, *Digital Literacy across the Curriculum: A Futurelab Handbook*, can be downloaded as a PDF at archive.futurelab.org.uk/resources/documents/handbooks/digital_literacy.pdf (accessed 31 October 2014).

References

Belshaw, D (2011) *What is 'Digital Literacy'?* [online] Available at: neverendingthesis.com/doug-belshaw-edd-thesis-final.pdf (accessed 31 October 2014).

Belshaw, D (2013) *Digital Literacies.* [online] Available at: www.slideshare.net/dajbelshaw/etmooc-t3-s1-digital-literacies-with-dr-doug-belshaw (accessed 31 October 2014).

Department for Education (2011) *Teachers' Standards: Guidance for School Leaders, School Staff and Governing Bodies.* [online] Available at: www.gov.uk/government/uploads/system/uploads/attachment_data/file/301107/Teachers__Standards.pdf (accessed 31 October 2014).

Department for Education (2013) *The National Curriculum in England: Framework Document.* [online] Available at: www.gov.uk/government/uploads/system/uploads/attachment_data/file/210969/NC_framework_document_-_FINAL.pdf (accessed 31 October 2014).

Facer, K (2009) *Educational, Social and Technological Futures: A Report from the Beyond Current Horizons Programme.* [online] Available at: www.beyondcurrenthorizons.org.uk/wp-content/uploads/final-report-2009.pdf (accessed 31 October 2014).

Hobbs, R (2010) *Digital and Media Literacy: A Plan of Action.* [online] Available at: www.knight-comm.org/wp-content/uploads/2010/12/Digital_and_Media_Literacy_A_Plan_of_Action.pdf (accessed 8 August 2014).

Joint Information Systems Committee (2014) *Developing Digital Literacies.* [online] Available at: www.jiscinfonet.ac.uk/whole-infokit/?infokit=11013 (accessed 31 October 2014).

Payton, S and Hague, C (2010) *Digital Literacy in Practice: Case Studies of Primary and Secondary Classrooms.* Futurelab. [online] Available at: www2.futurelab.org.uk/resources/documents/project_reports/digital_literacy_case_studies.pdf (accessed 31 October 2014).

Prensky, M (2001) Digital Natives, Digital Immigrants. [online] Available at: www.marcprensky.com/writing/Prensky%20-%20Digital%20Natives,%20Digital%20Immigrants%20-%20Part1.pdf (accessed 31 October 2014).

Puentedura, R (2013) The SAMR Framework. [online] Available at: edfutures.net/SAMR (accessed 31 October 2014).

Resnick, M (2012a) Reviving Papert's Dream. *Educational Technology,* 52(4): 42–6. [online] Available at: web.media.mit.edu/~mres/papers/educational-technology-2012.pdf (accessed 31 October 2014).

Resnick, M (2012b) Lifelong Kindergarten. *Cultures of Creativity*, pp 50–2. [online] Available at: web.media.mit.edu/~mres/papers/CulturesCreativityEssay.pdf (accessed 31 October 2014).

Resnick, M (2013) Teaching Kids to Code. [online] Available at: www.edsurge.com/n/2013-05-08-learn-to-code-code-to-learn (accessed 31 October 2014).

Ryberg, T and Georgsen, M (2010) Enabling Digital Literacy. *Nordic Journal of Digital Literacy*, 5(2): 88–100.

2 Implications for teaching: digital teaching

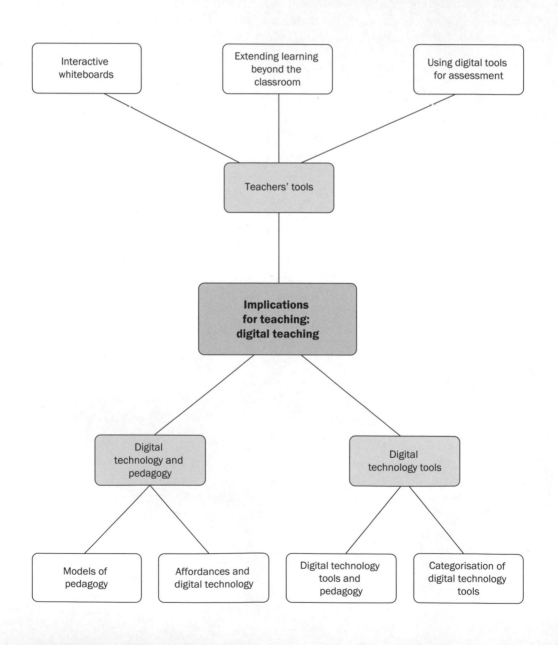

Interactive whiteboards

Extending learning beyond the classroom

Using digital tools for assessment

Teachers' tools

Implications for teaching: digital teaching

Digital technology and pedagogy

Digital technology tools

Models of pedagogy

Affordances and digital technology

Digital technology tools and pedagogy

Categorisation of digital technology tools

Introduction

The concepts of *digital natives* and *digital immigrants* are well known and familiar though what do these terms actually mean to you and how helpful are they in a teaching context? The popularised concept promoted by Marc Prensky (2001) emphasises the view that digital natives speak a digital language acquired as first language speakers. However, Helsper and Eynon (2010) refer to first and second generation digital natives (those born after 1980 and those born in the 1990s), and Tapscott (Rosenberg, 2014; Tapscott, 2009) referred to the *net generation* and *screenagers*; others have referred to generations X, Y and Z (Brown and Czerniewicz, 2010). Gardner and Davis (2013) focus on the rapid rate of technological change when noting that the time between generations is decreasing and opt for the *App Generation* as describing today's youth and their search for the super app to solve all life's challenges. Merzenich (2004) focused on the concept of *brain plasticity* which also suggests that a simple division between natives and immigrants is not quite as clear-cut as Prensky's original view would have us believe. As the title of danah boyd's book on the social lives of networked teens suggests, 'It's complicated' (2014).

Critical questions

» *Reflect critically and identify some strengths and weaknesses of the digital natives/ digital immigrants concept.*

» *Take a look at the National Archive of Educational Computing interactive timeline (www.naec.org.uk/events) and see how far back you can go before the technology context starts to lose its familiarity. How would you categorise yourself: screenager, millennial, generation X, Y or Z, App Generation?*

In 2014, numerous YouTube videos show babies and infants interacting with digital technology almost as if they were born with an innate digital technology ability not possessed by digital immigrants. However, the concept of affordances first introduced by Gibson (1986) suggests that design and intuitive ease of use of devices such as iPads have a large part to play in even the youngest children being able to learn without being specifically taught. A really good illustrative example is provided by the Hole in the Wall project (Mitra, 2007). Computers with internet access were installed literally into holes in walls in remote villages in India where children had hardly even seen a TV screen and who were in no sense of the word digital natives. Yet within a very short space of time and without any instruction at all children in the villages *picked up* how to open the browser and surf the internet, even learning how to speak English (the language of the internet) en route.

Critical question

Watch the Hole in the Wall video and use this to start reflecting on your view of teaching in the context of technology assisted learning. (Use the following link or search using the phrase kids can teach themselves.*)*

» *Do social constructivist models of learning with technology suggest a diminished role for the teacher? (www.ted.com/talks/sugata_mitra_shows_how_kids_teach_ themselves#t-1462)*

Digital technology and pedagogy

This section introduces you to theoretical perspectives which acknowledge the significance of digital technology within your approach to teaching.

Models of pedagogy

Although evidence based practice is a solid foundation for decisions relating to pedagogy it is important to recognise the complexity of teaching activity. Whether regarded as an art or science, as a holistic process or simply as influenced by a multiplicity of factors, sensory awareness, noticing, creative thinking and on-going reflection on practice are essential elements of effective pedagogy. Yet theoretical perspectives can help to focus attention and developments of Shulman's (1986) theory of teacher knowledge are useful in this regard. From Shulman's perspective teacher knowledge includes:

- subject knowledge (this relates to the subject you are teaching, so for computing this refers to the broad technological context and your personal digital technology capability, eg experience of computer programming or creating web pages);

- curriculum subject knowledge (this relates to the national curriculum subject you are teaching though may be cross-curricular, eg if teaching national curriculum computing do you know what an algorithm is?);

- general pedagogical knowledge (this relates to your awareness of teaching and learning theories);

- pedagogical content knowledge (see below);

- knowledge relating to learners and their characteristics (this relates to your awareness of such topics as child development, educational psychology but will also include awareness of children as inhabitants of a digital culture);

- knowledge of educational contexts (this is the wider context encompassed by educational policies, eg Byron Review);

- educational philosophy including aims and values (eg Chapter 7 asks you to think about the nature of education in the context of a rapidly changing digital world).

Essentially, teachers need to be clear about their aims, know the content of the curriculum subjects they are teaching, have an understanding of the nature of learning and also have knowledge of various dimensions of teaching, eg methods of teaching, classroom organisation and assessment. However, in addition to this, Shulman's model emphasises the importance of *pedagogical content knowledge* (Figure 2.1). This is the pedagogy specific to teaching particular subject content to particular learners, eg knowing the common misconceptions eight-year-old children have in the science topic of *forces* but also knowing specific teaching strategies to promote effective learning in *this* science topic with these children. Similarly, in the national curriculum for computing (DFE, 2013), knowing particular strategies for teaching the topic of digital citizenship (you can find out more about teaching digital citizenship by reading Chapter 7).

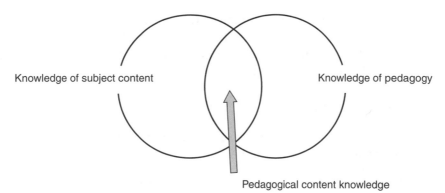

Figure 2.1 *Shulman's model*

Cogill's (2008) perspective valued Shulman's theory but recognised the changing nature of teacher knowledge and drew on theories which highlight practical wisdom including teachers' personal constructs and professional traditions. Cogill also recognised the importance of classroom events, observable practice, teachers' personal practical knowledge and, particularly in relation to pedagogical change, affordances of ICT. Cogill's theory is useful because it draws attention to the great complexity of teaching activity in which tacit knowledge and the practical wisdom of the teacher are significant elements of teacher knowledge. Teachers need to make many decisions each day in the concrete reality of the specific teaching context. It is consequently important to recognise the value of the Aristotelian concept of phronesis: practical wisdom. This is no less the case in relation to technology and the rapid pace of technological innovation and change in general. What may have been the case a year ago with version one of the software and hardware and with the children as they were then may not be the case now.

Mishra and Koehler (2006) gave particular attention to the significance of technology in their model of pedagogy. In particular they adapted Shulman's model to incorporate the influence of technology, referring to teacher knowledge as *technological pedagogical content knowledge* (TPCK) while also recognising other constituents as *technological content knowledge* and *technological pedagogical knowledge*. TPCK occurs where content, technology and pedagogy overlap. This is a particularly useful theory because it centres attention on the affordances of ICT. As an example consider teaching a primary science lesson where the learning outcomes relate to electrical circuits with a Year 5 class. The teacher will need appropriate curriculum and subject knowledge for the age group. It will be useful to have some awareness of the pupils' previous experience and common misconceptions. The teacher will also need to draw on general understanding of how children learn and strategies for managing the class. Where there are laptops available to the class and an Interactive Whiteboard, the teacher's *technological content knowledge* will comprise knowledge of affordances of appropriate software and features of the Interactive Whiteboard that may be useful for teaching about electrical circuits, eg simulation software where children can interact with the components on the computer, computer games relating to circuits and illustrative video clips. The teacher's *technological pedagogical knowledge* relates to the teacher's general knowledge of how to use the affordances of the technology to make the learning more effective. The teacher's TPCK will be the combined knowledge that includes being familiar with the software and what it has to offer the particular children being taught; knowing how to adapt the software and how to integrate the use of the software effectively into the lesson.

Critical questions

» *What have you learnt from your own experience of technology both within and outside the school context that can be useful when teaching?*

» *Analyse a lesson you have taught using Mishra and Koehler's model. Use the above example to identify the technological content knowledge and the technological pedagogical knowledge. How can this model help to improve the quality of teaching and learning?*

Affordances and digital technology

'Affordance' is a useful concept that draws attention to both enabling and constraining features of any object including digital technology tools and applications. It is the affordance of an object that provides the opportunity for action, eg a knife affords cutting and an iPad affords swiping, spreading and pressing movements that are within the capabilities of even very young children. A wide range of affordances have been identified in the literature as well as variations in the nature of the concept. Day and Lloyd (2007) refer to real and perceived affordances, simple affordances and complex affordances comprising nested and sequential affordances where one perceived affordance leads to the awareness of another, eg clicking on a menu item provides access to a submenu which provides access to other features of the software. They also refer to specific and general affordances and note that an object or ICT tool can have different affordances for different individuals.

Kennewell (2001) referred to the teacher's role as involving the need to make effective use of affordances and constraints in the school setting in relation to the abilities of the pupils. Kennewell's model is useful because it suggests the teacher needs to give less attention to alerting pupils to affordances and reduce constraints where pupils are finding the work activity too easy and vice versa. For example, searching the internet can be supported by reminding pupils of search strategies or demonstrating use of Boolean operators to draw attention to affordances of the search engine. However, the more able pupils may need less reminding. Similarly, if pupils are struggling to find what they are searching for, constraints can be introduced by the teacher such as specifying search phrases for the pupils to use.

Consideration of affordances allows for greater rationality when making decisions about use of technology in teaching. Well known affordances of digital technology include provisionality, speed and automatic functions, capacity, range and interactivity (DfEE, 1998). A few examples help to illustrate these affordances: the provisional nature of text in word processing software affords editing; databases allow for rapid retrieval of information; control technology can be used to automatically regulate the temperature; the great capacity of computer memory means that very detailed information can be accessed; the wide range of digital technologies affords different approaches to learning; and interactivity affords feedback whether from other contributors to a blog, from the image produced on the computer screen or from use of a computer assisted learning system. Conole and Dyke (2004) broaden the focus by drawing attention to both positive and negative affordances. Accessibility and speed of change are regarded as affordances of the information age/digital world. So much information is now available and change is occurring at such a phenomenal rate that information overload is a negative affordance. Pupils therefore need to develop digital literacy and become good digital citizens. Other affordances referred to by Conole and Dyke include diversity, communication and collaboration, reflection, multimodal non-linear, immediacy, surveillance, monopolisation, risk, fragility and uncertainty.

Critical question

» *Choose one piece of software or digital device. Identify its affordances and consider the implications of these affordances within a teaching context.*

Digital technology tools

This section provides you with a context for considering digital technology tools and extends the preceding focus on pedagogy. You are introduced to frameworks which provide a scaffold for considering the educational value of digital technology tools, including the idea of digital technology tools for teaching.

Digital technology tools and pedagogy

Software such as simulations and hardware such as Interactive Whiteboards are examples of digital technology tools and applications. Early frameworks such as *tutor*, *tool* and *tutee* (Taylor, 1980; Bull, 2009) were combined into the computer practice framework (CPF) by Twining (2002). However, the greater range of digital technologies that have emerged in recent years have led to revised versions of the CPF. In particular the Digital Technology Impact Framework (EdFutures, 2013a), Puentedura's (2013) SAMR model and the Education Innovation Framework (EdFutures, 2013b) highlight issues and encompass the broad range of digital technology. The models are based on three primary considerations: quantity, focus and mode.

Quantity

Quantity refers to extent of use of digital technology in an educational setting such as a school. Pertinent questions that you could ask would be how many computers and other digital devices are or should be available in the school, how frequently are they accessed or should be accessed and whether they should be used one-to-one or for group learning. Cuban's (2001) book *Oversold and Underused* draws attention to the theme of technological determinism and argues that simply having technology available does not mean it is having an impact on pupils' achievement. You need to make effective use of technology if it's going to have any impact on learning. Having the most up-to-date technology may impress the parents but may be of little value where the installed software is inappropriate or where teachers lack confidence and the IT capability to use it. Loveless (1995) identified a *conjectural* use of technology as one of four modes which also included emancipatory, revelatory and instructional uses. Conjecture is a form of reflective thinking that can be developed effectively through group discussion. For example, you could provide a group of pupils with a spreadsheet model or a control technology problem to interpret and analyse by a bouncing ideas off each other. McKenzie (2002) referred to collaboration as a pedagogical principle supporting effective learning; and also emphasised the value of *just in time* equipment in preference to *just in case* equipment (McKenzie, 2001). A large investment in new technology can bring pressure to use the technology but without good reason. A simple rule of thumb that you can use when planning a lesson is to consider the potential of the technology for improving the quality of the pupils' learning.

Focus

Focus separates use of digital technology into the three categories of computing, information and communication technology (ICT) and other. The focus on ICT specifically refers to technology enhanced learning where digital technology is used to support learning in other curriculum subjects. This is where the aim of using ICT is to have an impact on the quality of the pupils' learning. For example, the Interactive Whiteboard can be used to enhance the teaching of science. The first two categories relate directly to the national curriculum (DFE, 2013). The focus on *other uses* includes anything else, eg enhancing the public image of the school.

Mode

Mode specifically refers to the type of impact or potential impact of ICT on learning using the terms *support*, *enhance* and *transform*. Authors such as Seymour Papert (1998) have been very critical of the nineteenth-century factory model of education that has persisted into the twenty-first century. Although the concepts of *ostrich*, *techno-ostrich* and *cyberostriches* conjure amusing images, eg of a horse and cart being powered by a jet engine, Papert's intention is to demonstrate the absurdity of trying to fit new technology into an old way of life.

> *I give the title of ostrich to educators who are excited by the prospect that computers will improve what they do in schools but hide their heads in the sand to avoid seeing that these technologies will inexorably give rise to megachange that goes far beyond improvement.*
>
> (Papert, 1996, p 24)

The image is one of learning being *supported* by technology but without any fundamental changes to curriculum or pedagogy. In order for technology to *enhance* learning on the other hand you may need to make changes to your pedagogical approach and interpretation of the curriculum. This helps cast some light on the meaning of *transform* which refers to the type of impact on curriculum and pedagogy that can only really occur because of the use of digital technology.

Loveless et al (2001) contrasted *old pedagogy* with *new pedagogy*. Although some of the *old pedagogy* is now truly old, eg that related to '*Know as much as there is in the book and as much as the teacher says*' (p 80), some other forms of old pedagogy still persist, eg '*Teacher uses lecture to pass on his or her knowledge to the students*' (p 80) and can be supported by technology such as a microphone to amplify the voice of the teacher. An Interactive Whiteboard might also be used but in the capacity of an ordinary chalk-board. Puentedura (2013), in the SAMR framework, refers to this way of utilising digital technology as **S**ubstitution. On the other hand, some of the *new technology* is now well established, eg that related to '*Intellectual product has a professional look printed with colour and attention to design*'. Puentedura (2013) refers to this way of utilising digital technology as **A**ugmentation. However, *transformed* learning, such as live interaction unbounded by classroom walls or using data loggers for continuous monitoring of changes to the classroom environment, can only be achieved through the use of technology. Bloom's digital taxonomy of knowledge (Churches, 2014) helps focus attention on technology transformed learning in the digital world by recognising knowledge creation at the summit of the hierarchy, eg the collaborative learning made possible through use of an online wiki. The SAMR framework characterises transformation using the concepts of '**R**edefinition *– Tech allows for the creation of new tasks, previously inconceivable*' and '**M**odification *– Tech allows for significant task redesign*'. This is reflected by Selinger and Kaye (2014) when considering digital technology tools and applications categorised as used for consumption or production.

Categorisation of digital technology tools

With hundreds of potentially relevant tools and applications to choose from, categorising can help you identify those that you can use to support, enhance or transform learning within any particular lesson. Developing familiarity with the affordances of a range of tools will help to increase your technological content knowledge and will be useful for curriculum planning and development. Selinger and Kaye (2014) used a simple approach that positions pupils as consumers or producers. This relates well to the rationale of the new computing curriculum which supports the view that pupils should not just be end users, eg although they should have the capability to play video games they should also learn how to create the games as well. Tools supporting pupils as consumers include internet resources that pupils can use for researching a topic; presentation hardware and software that teachers can use such as Interactive Whiteboards and related software; and simulations and games that pupils can use to learn in a more interactive way, including integrated learning systems. Tools supporting pupils as producers include the computing part of the curriculum such as programming with Logo, Scratch, 2Code, Kodu game lab and Alice. The emphasis on pupils as producers can also be recognised in the wide range of tools and Web 2.0 tools associated with the creation category of Bloom's digital taxonomy (Churches, 2014). Web 2.0 tools are the particular focus of Chapter 6.

An alternative way of categorising is to group tools used by pupils and tools used by teachers. Although there is inevitably an overlap and merging of boundaries, eg Interactive Whiteboards can be used by both pupils and teachers, teachers' tools include the use of digital technology for communicating subject knowledge, assessment, feedback and extending learning beyond the classroom and school day. The range of software and online apps within each tool type is extensive, eg the Centre for Learning and Performance Technologies (CLPT, 2014) lists more than 2000 examples of software and applications including those specifically related to various aspects of the teacher's role such as instructional tools, presentation creation tools, virtual classroom and discussion forum tools, polling and survey tools as well as personal productivity tools.

Critical questions

»   *In relation to quantity, do an audit of technology in your school including what technology is available and frequency of use. Identify any issues relating to quantity.*

»   *Look back on some of your recent teaching: can you identify ways in which you have used technology to support, enhance and transform the learning experience?*

»   *Transformation for its own sake will not improve the quality of your teaching or your pupils' learning. How might digital technology help you transform your teaching in a way that does enhance pupils' learning?*

Teachers' tools

The following sections focus on teaching points and themes related to use of Interactive Whiteboards, extending learning beyond the school day and using ICT for assessment at the level of technological pedagogical and technological content knowledge.

Interactive whiteboards

The interactive whiteboard (IW) may be a Promethean board which uses a magnetic pen or a pressure-sensitive SMART board. More recent SMART boards allow multi-touch capability for simultaneous use by two users and support gesturing such as zooming and rotating. The advantages of the magnetic pen are that users can rest their arm or hand on the board when writing and using the pen avoids contact with sticky fingers. Another factor to consider in relation to choice and installation is the location of the IW which should be away from direct exposure to reflected light. An adjustable height IW will make the board accessible for pupils to use. The SMART notebook and ActivInspire software should also be considered, ie with regard to the extensive range of affordances offered by the software including ease of use.

The IW supports whole class, group and individual teaching and learning approaches. As a generic tool you can use the IW to show websites, images and video clips (subject to copyright); for *PowerPoint*, *Prezzi*, *Google slides* or other presentation software; to enhance the start or plenary of the lesson; and also to support assessment. You can use annotation tools to add and save notes that can be returned to later in the lesson or for revision during a follow-up lesson. Tools such as the *spotlight* tool can be used to zoom in on a particular part of the screen, engaging the pupils through questioning and discussion while gradually revealing the complete image. Cogill (2006, p 13) suggested the interesting idea, in relation to Assessment for Learning, of enlarging '*a spreadsheet for children to self-monitor their understanding of the [lesson] objectives*' though sensitivity would be needed if progress of individual children was visible to the whole class.

Research by Marzano (2009) indicated that IWs can have a positive impact on pupils' attainment. For example, if you give every child in your class a hand-held voting device (part of the ActiVote system which records responses) you are then able to probe individual pupils' responses. Another main contributor to increased attainment identified by Marzano is the multimodal support provided by the IW, again provided that you don't obscure the main content by images and/or other multimedia and maintain an appropriate pace. A third statistically significant improvement to attainment was correlated with using the IW to reinforce learning, eg you could use *virtual applause* as a reward for the correct answer. However, Marzano advised teachers to ensure pupils understand why their answer is the correct one and emphasised that as *'with all powerful tools, teachers must use interactive whiteboards thoughtfully, in accordance with what we know about good classroom practice'*.

You can also use the IW to support and enhance small group and even individual use by pupils. Fogarty (2012) found that IWs can be a more effective tool for small group collaborative learning than collaboration using laptops. Warwick and Mercer (2011) emphasised the importance of the scaffolding provided by the IW for the learning activity and drew attention to the need to teach pupils how to work collaboratively in small groups in order to maximise the potential for effective learning.

It's the way you use the technology, rather than technology per se, that makes it potentially facilitative of pupils learning effectively. Hennessy (2011) argued that the IW is a new form of cultural tool providing new opportunities for transforming learning:

> *Its particular affordances, including visibility, provisionality, stability, direct manipulation, multimodality, and re-usability, potentially offer strong support for cumulative, collaborative, and recursive learning.*
>
> (p 483)

Through use of the IW teachers and pupils are able to work collaboratively, manipulating provisional mediating digital artefacts, eg images, video clips, text, clip art and on-screen annotations in order to *'draw learners into new forms and spaces of productive dialogue'* (p 467).

Critical questions

» *In order to move away from a replacement way of using the IW as a conventional whiteboard, try out some of the IW tools that you haven't yet used and reflect on the outcomes.*

» *Plan, teach and reflect on a lesson using one or more of these IW tools in a way that helps to enhance or transform your teaching.*

Extending learning beyond the classroom

Current research suggests that until recently digital technology (including school learning platforms, intranets, use of email and text message contact with parents, as well as netbooks loaned to families) has had limited impact on improving parental engagement. The research by Selwyn et al (2011) for example suggested that although some parents have felt a greater sense of involvement, there has been a low level of use by parents and no use at all by parents with no internet access. However, Selwyn et al (2011) note:

> *This previous lack of impact notwithstanding, as the 2010s progress growing efforts are being made both from within schools and from national and regional policymakers to encourage the coordinated and systematic use of digital technologies to support parent-school engagement.*
>
> (p 315)

Typical uses of a school's virtual learning environment (VLE) is to keep parents informed of school events and news items; to showcase pupils' achievements; and to communicate information to parents about their child's homework, attendance, behaviour and attainment. When used in this way the VLE has the potential to build on and enhance the usual process of keeping parents informed, including round-the-clock access. Instead of contact being the scheduled termly parents' evening, parents are able to monitor their child's progress on a more frequent basis. They are also able to keep track of and potentially become more involved with homework activities, a role which is particularly important for supporting children's progress. The school's VLE also helps to maintain contact with hard-to-reach parents, eg those with physical disabilities. However, teachers have expressed heightened awareness of accountability and noted the impact of their increased visibility on their professional role.

Selwyn et al (2011) drew attention to the predominantly *top-down* approach to using the VLE in which schools convey information to parents. They refer to the current typical use of VLEs as *institutional technologies* which position the parents as receivers rather than as active participants. If new digital technologies are going to do more than '*reflect and reinforce – rather than reconfigure – existing patterns of school/parent engagement*' (p 323) then schools need to foster more of a partnership perspective rather than simply communicating the school's message to the parents. Following on from this theme, Grant (2011) identified a separation between home and school cultures and focused on the need to develop a *third space*, where children can realise the combined value of their *funds of knowledge* from home and school.

Particularly in relation to preschool and very young children where play is the primary form of learning, the VLE can extend access to online software that children enjoy playing with at school. Parents are able to enjoy the experience of being a part of the child's learning where their child is already familiar with use of the software. This is illustrated by one of the many video clips related to engaging parents through use of VLEs (nextgenlearning, 2009). And not just in the early years but throughout the primary school and beyond, there are many opportunities for using the VLE to transform the approach to learning and teaching:

- use of e-portfolios within the VLE allows not only teachers but also parents to upload evidence relating to the progress of individual children;

- video clips of children working and/or examples of children's work can be used for review, eg by child and parents when at home as well as by teacher and child during the school day;

- the VLE provides an opportunity to perceive learning as a continuous anytime, anywhere process;

- pupils are brought into contact with a wider audience;

- transition between key stages is facilitated;

- *learning loss* can be reduced during long summer holidays through fun and engaging educational activities uploaded to the VLE for when children want to continue with their learning;

- a blog space within the VLE provides a potentially valuable discussion area for both parents and teachers.

The focus on home–school relations is part of the more recent personalisation agenda which includes encouraging children's engagement in personally meaningful learning outside the school context. If parents are simply expected to support the school's agenda, this can be counterproductive and alienating for both parents and children. The focus needs to be on enhancing the quality of parental engagement in children's learning.

Critical question

> A useful question to focus attention, one of several from the Futurelab report 'Developing the home-school relationship using digital technologies' (Grant, 2010, p 59) is 'How can schools engage with parents and children in a more explicit process of negotiation and consultation to develop clear, shared expectations of one another?'

Using digital tools for assessment

It's recognised that providing learners with constructive feedback helps improve attainment. It's also recognised that metacognitive skills relating to self-assessment help make learning more effective. This is visible in the Teaching Standards (DFE, 2011) Q6d: 'Give pupils regular feedback, both orally and through accurate marking, and encourage pupils to respond to the feedback.' Q6 also identifies the need to make effective use of a variety of assessment strategies. ICT applications can help with the attainment of these standards because of the inbuilt feedback features of software applications. For example, a word processor typically underlines a spelling and/or grammatical error; instructional software may include pop-up prompts with helpful guidance on how to answer a question posed by the software. The integrated learning system (ILS) 'SuccessMaker' (Pearson, no date) which incorporates scaffolded feedback within a customised learning environment, is supported by extensive research suggesting its positive impact on performance.

Collecting evidence of children's progress for both formative and summative purposes can be time consuming, involve lots of photocopying and include a disorganised collection of notes that are lost even before they reach the child's record folder. Of course, children's progress is not confined to work produced on paper and collecting evidence of non-paper based work can be problematic. Using ICT tools for assessment can help you address each of these challenges. A digital image, a short video clip or audio recording of a child talking to other group members during a science investigation can be stored in a digital portfolio record of the child's progress. You can also set up a spreadsheet to record assessment data which can be useful for showing trends through use of the charting features. A simple practical idea that you can try out is to create a *PowerPoint* template for each child with sections for each subject area, including a copy of NC objectives for each subject in the notes area which you can then match to digitised evidence such as photos of work and audio clips; this could also be included within the VLE and made available to the parents.

A particularly useful software application specifically intended for assessment, produced by 2 Simple software, is called 2Build a Profile (available from www.2simple.com/apps). Versions exist for both the Early Years Foundation Stage and also for Key Stages 1 and 2.

A review by an Early Years Foundation Stage co-ordinator, Chere (2013), emphasised how it helped reduce time for collecting and organising evidence, reduced printing costs, was easy to use, allowed data from multiple devices to be automatically synchronised, and also valued the option to email parents with regular progress reports. One approach to integrating 2Build a Profile within an early years setting has been for staff to carry iPads with them throughout the day. This simple extension of usual early years practice allows instant tagging of photos or video clips to the appropriate learning goals within a child's profile.

Critical questions

» *How is ICT being used to support assessment in your setting?*

» *How might you maximise the potential of ICT for supporting assessment in your setting?*

Critical points

» *Reflect on images of youth purveyed through the media and compare with recent research in order to arrive at a less stereotypical view.*

» *Use the further reading section to explore and evaluate theories of pedagogy that include recognition of the digital technology context of learning and teaching. Consider how these theories can help improve the quality of teaching and learning.*

» *Revisit the concept of affordances in order to reflect further on ways to enhance pupils' learning.*

Further reading and useful resources

• Prensky popularised the concept of digital natives/immigrants way back in 2000. This is still a hot topic with plenty of recent publications to choose from. For example, the following are all very useful perspectives to consider:

 – Davies, C and Eynon, R (2013) *Teenagers and Technology*. London: Routledge.

 – Gardner, H and Davis, K (2013) *The App Generation*. London: Yale University Press.

 – Boyd, D (2014) *It's Complicated: The Social Life of Networked Teens*. London: Yale University Press.

 – Reading the articles written by Cogill (2008) and Mishra and Koehler (2006) would help you think more deeply about their models of pedagogy.

• The categorisation of digital technology tools included tools for supporting pupils as producers.

 – Scratch is available online at scratch.mit.edu/.

 – Kodu Game Lab can be downloaded from www.kodugamelab.com/.

 – Logo can be downloaded from el.media.mit.edu/logo-foundation/.

 – Alice can be downloaded from www.alice.org/index.php.

References

Boyd, D (2014) *It's Complicated: The Social Lives of Networked Teens*. London: Yale University Press.

Brown, C and Czerniewicz, L (2010) Debunking the 'Digital Native': Beyond Digital Apartheid, towards Digital Democracy. *Journal of Computer Assisted Learning*, 26: 357–69.

Bull, G (2009) Tutor, tool, tutee: a vision revisited. [online] Available at:www.citejournal.org/articles/v9i2editorial1.pdf (accessed 31 October 2014).

Centre for Learning and Performance Technologies (CLPT) (2014) Tools Directory. [online] Available at: c4lpt.co.uk/directory-of-learning-performance-tools/ (accessed 31 October 2014).

Chere, R (2013) 2Build a Profile – Case Study. [online] Available at: www.childcareexpo.co.uk/m-news/view/2build-a-profile-%E2%80%93-case-study(3221).htm (accessed 31 October 2014).

Churches, A (2014) Bloom's Digital Taxonomy. [online] Available at:edorigami.wikispaces.com/file/view/bloom%27s+Digital+taxonomy+v3.01.pdf/65720266/bloom%27s%20Digital%20taxonomy%20v3.01.pdf (accessed 31 October 2014).

Cogill, J (2006) *You Can Use an Interactive Whiteboard. For Ages 4–7*. London: Scholastic.

Cogill, J (2008) Pedagogy and Models of Teacher Knowledge. [online] Available at: juliecogill.com/Chapter_2.pdf (accessed 31 October 2014).

Conole, G and Dyke, M (2004) What are the Affordance Risks of Information and Communication Technologies? Paper presented at BERA anuual conference, Heriot-Watt University, Edinburgh, 11–13 September 2003. [online] Available at: repository.alt.ac.uk/596/1/ALT_J_Vol12_No2_2004_What%20are%20the%20affordances%20of%20in.pdf (accessed 31 October 2014).

Cuban, L (2001) *Oversold and Underused*. London: Harvard University Press.

Day, D and Lloyd, M (2007) Affordances of Online Technologies: More than the Properties of the Technology. *Australian Educational Computing*, 22(2): 17–21.

Department for Education (2011) *Teachers' Standards: Guidance for School Leaders, School Staff and Governing Bodies*. [online] Available at: www.gov.uk/government/uploads/system/uploads/attachment_data/file/301107/Teachers__Standards.pdf (accessed 31 October 2014).

Department for Education (2013) *The National Curriculum in England: Framework Document*. [online] Available at: www.gov.uk/government/uploads/system/uploads/attachment_data/file/239033/PRIMARY_national_curriculum_-_Computing.pdf (accessed 31 October 2014).

DfEE (1998) *Requirements for Courses of Initial Teacher Training, Circular number 4/98*. London: Teacher Training Agency (TTA).

EdFutures (2013a) Digital Technology Impact Framework. [online] Available at: edfutures.net/DTIF (accessed 31 October 2014).

EdFutures (2013b) The Education Innovation Framework. [online] Available at: edfutures.net/EdIF (accessed 31 October 2014).

Fogarty, I (2012) [online] Available at: downloads01.smarttech.com/media/research/international_research/canada/11_0142_new%20brunswick_research_summary.pdf (accessed 31 October 2014).

Gardner, H and Davies, K (2013) *The App Generation*. London: Yale University Press.

Gibson, J J (1986) The Theory of Affordances. [online] Available at: courses.media.mit.edu/2004spring/mas966/Gibson%20Theory%20of%20Affordances.pdf (accessed 31 October 2014).

Grant, L (2010) Developing the Home-School Relationship using Digital Technologies. Futurelab. [online] Available at: archive.futurelab.org.uk/resources/documents/handbooks/home-school_relationships.pdf (accessed 31 October 2014).

Grant, L (2011) 'I'm a completely different person at home': Using Digital Technologies to Connect Learning between Home and School. *Journal of Computer Assisted Learning*, 27: 292–302.

Helsper, W J and Eynon, R (2010) Digital Natives: Where is the Evidence? *British Educational Research Journal*, 36(3): 503–20.

Hennessy, S (2011) The Role of Digital Artefacts on the Interactive Whiteboard in Supporting Classroom Dialogue. *Journal of Computer Assisted Learning*, 27(6): 463–89.

Kennewell, S (2001) Using Affordances and Constraints to Evaluate the Use of Information and Communications Technology in Teaching and Learning. *Journal of Information Technology for Teacher Education*, 10(1–2): 101–16.

Loveless, A (1995) *The Role of IT: Practical Issues for the Primary Teacher*. London: Cassell.

Loveless, A, DeVoogd, G and Bohlin, R (2001) Something old, something new...: is pedagogy affected by ICT? in Loveless, A and Ellis, V (eds) *ICT, Pedagogy and the Curriculum*. London: Routledge-Falmer.

Marzano R (2009) [online] Available at: educ615sx.wikispaces.com/file/view/Marzano%20Whiteboards.pdf/434842880/Marzano%20Whiteboards.pdf (accessed 31 October 2014).

McKenzie, J (2001) Just in Time Technology. [online] Available at: fno.org/sept01/toolishness.html (accessed 31 October 2014).

McKenzie, J (2002) Is Sharing Out of the Question. [online] Available at: www.fno.org/apr02/sharing.html (accessed 31 October 2014).

Merzenich, M (2004) [online] Available at: www.ted.com/talks/michael_merzenich_on_the_elastic_brain (accessed 31 October 2014).

Mishra, P and Koehler, M (2006) Technological Pedagogical Content Knowledge: A Framework for Teacher Knowledge. *Teachers College Record*, 108(6): 1017–54. [online] Available at: punya.educ.msu.edu/publications/journal_articles/mishra-koehler-tcr2006.pdf (accessed 31 October 2014).

Mitra, S (2007) Kids Can Teach Themselves. TED Talks. [online] Available at: www.ted.com/talks/sugata_mitra_shows_how_kids_teach_themselves#t-1462 (accessed 31 October 2014).

National Archive of Educational Computing (NAEC) (no date) [online] Available at: www.naec.org.uk/ (accessed 31 October 2014).

nextgenlearning (2009) [online] Available at: www.youtube.com/watch?v=U78ZmhquRvw&feature=relmfu (accessed 31 October 2014).

Papert, S (1996) *The Connected Family*. Atlanta: Longstreet Press.

Papert, S (1998) Child Power: Keys to the New Learning of the Digital Century. [online] Available at: www.papert.org/articles/Childpower.html (accessed 31 October 2014).

Pearson (no date) [online] Available at: www.pearsonschool.com/index.cfm?locator=PS24Tj (accessed 31 October 2014).

Prensky, M (2001) Digital Natives, Digital Immigrants. [online] Available at: www.marcprensky.com/writing/Prensky%20-%20Digital%20Natives,%20Digital%20Immigrants%20-%20Part1.pdf (accessed 31 October 2014).

Puentedura, R (2013) The SAMR Framework. [online] Available at: edfutures.net/SAMR (accessed 31 October 2014).

Rosenberg, S (2014) Raised on the Net. [online] Available at: www.units.miamioh.edu/psybersite/cyberspace/n-gen/tapscott.shtml (accessed 31 October 2014).

Selinger, M and Kaye, L (2014) ICT Tools and Applications, in Leask, M and Pachler, N (eds) *Learning to Teach Using ICT in the Secondary School*. London: Routledge, pp 84–100.

Selwyn, N, Banaji, S, Hadjithoma-Garstka, C and Clark, W (2011) Providing a Platform for Parents? Exploring the Nature of Parental Engagement with School Learning Platforms. *Journal of Computer Assisted Learning*, 27: 314–23.

Shulman, L (1986) Those Who Understand: Knowledge Growth in Teaching. *Educational Researcher*, 15(2): 4–14. [online] Available at:www.fisica.uniud.it/URDF/masterDidSciUD/materiali/pdf/Shulman_1986.pdf (accessed 31 October 2014).

Tapscott, D (2009) *Grown Up Digital*. London: McGraw Hill.

Taylor, RP (1980) The Computer in School: Tutor, Tool, Tutee. [online] Available at:www.citejournal.org/vol3/iss2/seminal/article1.cfm (accessed 31 October 2014).

Twining, P (2002) Conceptualising Computer Use in Education: Introducing the Computer Practice Framework. *British Educational Research Journal*, 28(1): 95–110.

Warwick, P and Mercer, N (2011) Using the Interactive Whiteboard to Scaffold Pupils' Learning of Science in Colloaborative Group Activity. [online] Available at: iwbcollaboration.educ.cam.ac.uk/publications/Scaffolding-symposium-paper-for-website.pdf (accessed 31 October 2014).

3 Implications for learning: digital learning

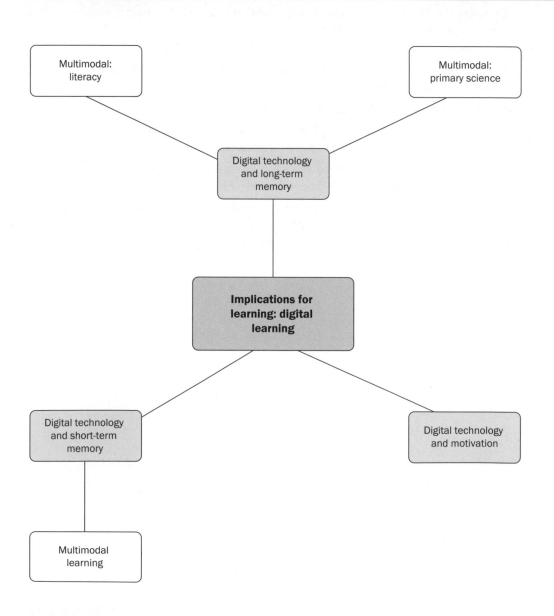

Multimodal: literacy

Multimodal: primary science

Digital technology and long-term memory

Implications for learning: digital learning

Digital technology and short-term memory

Digital technology and motivation

Multimodal learning

Introduction

As long ago as 1998 Seymour Papert, the inventor of the Logo computer language for children, expressed the view that the education system was far behind the times, a factory system where pupils are batched and processed en masse. He continued his lecture by illustrating how '*information technology, how digital technology, can provide a kind of infrastructure for Dewey's ideas that was not available until now*' (Papert, 1998). Papert's constructionist views can be seen as one of the forebears of valuing a more personalised curriculum and approach to teaching. As explained more recently by Green et al (2005) personalisation involves responding to the learning needs of pupils as individuals:

> *a system capable of offering bespoke support for each individual that recognises and builds upon the diverse strengths, interests, abilities and needs in order to foster engaged and independent learners able to reach their full potential.*
>
> (p 3)

As pupils grow older and start to take their place in the world as individuals with their own interests and values, digital technology can help them make informed choices. The more opportunities you give pupils to experience an extended range of digital technology such as film and photo editing, sound recording, web page creation, computer simulations and so on, the more opportunity the pupils will have to discover what really interests them as well as helping them evaluate tools for independent learning. The focus on pupils learning to make informed choices is also supported by the NAACE (2001) discussion document which includes *autonomy*, children choosing how they approach the learning activity, as one of the key features of effective teaching and learning. Less prescriptive activities can enable pupils to use their developing digital literacy capability and to have greater ownership of the task. For example, if you plan autonomous learning into a history/geography project some pupils might decide to use a digital camera to take photos, others might choose to use a sound recorder to interview the caretaker who has worked at the school for many years. Some might choose to create their project report using *PowerPoint* whereas others might decide to create a poster. Providing a supportive learning environment in this way can encourage children's intrinsic motivation and deep learning as children get really involved in developing their own approaches and ideas.

Another way that you can increase the learning value for the pupils, in addition to creating a sense of ownership, is to increase the authenticity of the learning experience (Herrington and Kervin, 2007; McFarlane, 1997). Providing an authentic context and an authentic activity is a useful first step and this might include pupils identifying the audience and responding to a real world issue. For example, maybe litter and untidiness is identified as an issue at the school. What can class four do to respond to this issue? Pupils might decide to take photos and produce a series of annotated posters for display in key areas. They might also decide to produce a slide presentation to be located in the entrance area of the school including interview extracts with staff members and children from other classes. They might even create a *Take Care of Our School* video to be shown at a whole school assembly. This is potentially a great opportunity to develop a creative approach to teaching and learning.

Critical questions

Child-centred rather than curriculum-centred approaches have firm roots in the views of educational philosophers such as John Dewey (StateUniversity.com, 2014) and well known reports such as the Plowden Report (1967).

» *How can you enable learners 'to have a sense of ownership and control over their own learning at the same time as encouraging them to explore new and unfamiliar areas?' (Green et al, 2005, p 15).*

» *Identify and evaluate a particular lesson where you have given (or could give) children the opportunity to decide for themselves how to use digital technology to help achieve the learning objectives.*

Digital technology and short-term memory

The media in September 2009 included headlines such as 'Video war games "boost working memory"' (Sky News, 2009). The details noted that Facebook and Sudoku were also good for strengthening the short-term working memory whereas *'text messaging, micro-blogging on Twitter, and watching YouTube were all likely to weaken "working memory"'*. Of course this was not long after the publication of the Byron Review (2008) which had raised awareness about *'potentially inappropriate material'* (Byron, 2008, p 2) but the focus on developing memory was an important one. A few minutes thought about the short-term working memory suggests the potential impact on learning. For example, in relation to teaching strategies, if you show pupils a lengthy animation of cloud formation followed by a verbal explanation this may not be the best option as some of the content of the animation is likely to be forgotten and won't be associated with your verbal explanation.

Moreno and Mayer (2000) elaborated implications of the short-term working memory in their cognitive theory of multimedia learning. This assigns a key role for the working memory in relation to selecting, organising and integrating sensory data. Their research provided evidence for six principles for promoting effective learning underpinned by the assumption that the short-term working memory comprises independent areas for auditory and visual working memory. It's worth taking a look at these principles as they provide some useful insights for lesson planning and for preparing teaching resources.

The first principle, *split-attention*, reinforces the view that if you present content in only one modality (eg visual or auditory) overload may occur in that modality whereas other modalities are available but not being used. Think about subtitles when watching a foreign language film: the action has moved on by the time you have read the subtitle. Now think about a computer simulation of an eclipse, such as might be shown to a Key Stage 2 class in a science lesson. If a text explanation is shown on the screen at the same time as the animation, then attention will need to be split between reading the text and watching the animation so quality of learning is likely to be reduced. On the other hand, if you were to narrate the animation (or if you had a concurrent audio explanation) then both the visual and auditory working memories would be used.

Critical questions

» *Would it be better to show an animation with both the text explanation visible on screen and an audio explanation? Explain your answer.*

» *What's likely to be the impact of including extraneous sound effects?*

» *Would it make any difference if you integrated explanatory text into the animation or visual image (eg speech bubbles) rather than showing this on a separate part of the screen?*

» *Would it be better to show text on screen while also reading this text aloud?*

(NB Moreno and Mayer's split-attention principle, spatial contiguity principle, coherence principle *and* redundancy principle *are useful for answering these questions. You can read the article by following the link in the suggested further reading.)*

Multimodal learning

It's useful to contrast multimedia with multimodal even though these concepts may have previously been used interchangeably. *Multimedia* refers specifically to the medium, eg digital or physical used to contain the message. In other words the same information may be communicated in a digitised version of a newspaper or in a duplicated physical copy. Of course, some people may prefer to physically hold the paper than look at the computer screen. In the case of an old map, an old book or an antique, being able to make actual physical contact may contribute to the value. Using graphics software will enable effects that it's not otherwise possible to produce, which can also add to the value of using different media. *Multimodal* on the other hand refers to the different forms of communication regardless of the medium. Moreno and Mayer (2000) specifically separate sensory data into auditory and visual modalities and Cisco (2008) grouped visual, tactile, gustatory and olfactory data in relation to the way in which the short-term working memory deals with different modalities. However, the concept of modality is broader than this and originates in the study of social semiotics (Kress, 2010). A few minutes' thought brings a range of modalities into view, eg a *descriptive* modality could include use of speech, graphics, text, tables and charts and a *figurative* modality could include analogies, metaphors and images. Murcia (2010) identified *descriptive, experimental, mathematical, figurative* and *kinaesthetic* modalities (p 24).

Moreno and Mayer (2000) explain the 'modality principle' in relation to the short-term working memory: essentially it's more effective if you present content using more than one modality (eg visual as well as auditory). For example, showing part of the eclipse animation followed by a short textual explanation (to avoid the cognitive overload of concurrent animation and text) then more of the animation followed by text explanation, is still less effective than including a verbal explanation for pupils to listen to.

Digital technology and long-term memory

Effective learning requires attention to both short-term and long-term memory. As a teacher you will want to empower your pupils to do more than simply be able to recall details for a test at the end of the day or week. Of course, you might take the alternative view that cultivating the long-term memory is of less value in today's world with the ever-increasing capacities of computer hard drives and the almost infinite capacity of the internet. Do we really need examinations which test longer term retention of content? In fact, how much do we really need to rely on our long-term memories if information can be stored even more efficiently and recovered super rapidly using a search engine? If computers can reduce the memory burden won't that free up the brain's resources and enable it to function more effectively? Maybe ... but then it's also worth considering Carr's (2011) explanation of the dissimilarity between the functioning of the human memory which he describes as creative and organic and the computer memory which is a static collection of small bits of data. In other words ideas can grow and evolve from human memories whereas computers only organise and reorganise bits of unchanging data. Whether or not you believe in the value of testing long-term memory learning for life involves adaptability, transferable skills and being able to draw on previous experience which is part of the value of studying history. There's always going to be value in cultivating the long-term memory.

Research evidence suggests you may need to think carefully about use of digital technology in relation to long-term memory. For example, as previously suggested, the rapid flow of information can create cognitive overload so that very little information actually reaches the long-term memory. However, even more significantly, several studies refer to the rewiring of the brain as a consequence of extended exposure to digital media. Carr (2011) in particular refers to several studies that provide evidence for the diminished capacity of the human brain to organise information, focus attention and think deeply due to continued frequent use of digital media. However, Miller (2009) identified several principles for improving the long-term memory together with some ideas for how digital technology can play a supportive role.

- The *testing effect*: testing yourself on what you are learning is a good way of improving your long-term memory. One example of this is where you get the children to close their books from time to time and test themselves to see if they can recall details. Digital technology can be a highly motivating alternative: automatically generated online quizzes can enable pupils to make repeated attempts as many times as they like (and also while at home).

- The *spacing effect*: trying to do everything all at once is less effective than learning a little bit at a time with a space in between. In other words cramming might help you get through the exam but the material being learnt is soon forgotten afterwards. A gradual approach where different steps are reinforced and reviewed is likely to be more effective for longer term learning. This is where you teach children to save, edit and review their *Word* document. Pupils can also make effective use of instructional technology such as educational computer games as these typically divide the learning activity into separate parts and levels, and often include time out activities in-between the more focused learning tasks. You could also use the school's virtual learning environment (VLE) to support the spacing effect by creating activities for pupils to continue learning beyond the lesson.

- The *adaptive memory effect*: memory improves when the need to remember is perceived to be important for satisfying future needs and longer term survival. This suggests the value of personalisation of the curriculum and is pursued further in the following section on motivation.

Another point worth considering is whether the technology has the appropriate affordances for the task. For example, *Time* magazine (2012) emphasised that it can take several attempts to remember content in an e-book compared to a printed text so may not be the best choice '*when you want to study complex ideas and concepts that you wish to integrate deeply into your memory*'. Research studies have also questioned the impact of reading electronic texts on comprehension. Jabr (2013) noted '*even so-called digital natives are more likely to recall the gist of a story when they read it on paper because enhanced e-books and e-readers themselves are too distracting. Paper's greatest strength may be its simplicity*'. So it's worth reflecting on the design of electronic media, eg is the e-book simply a direct copy of the printed text or is it a well-designed e-book? Moreover, Jones (2013, 2014) is critical of Jabr's findings, recognises the complexity of the issues surrounding printed texts versus electronic texts and argues positively that '*the research underscores the need for digital literacy instruction; that is, how to use their tools in a way that serves their learning goals*'.

Short-term and long-term memory are two important factors that you need to focus on in order to promote effective learning. Of course there are also a range of other significant factors that you need to consider, some of which were highlighted by the Cisco report on multimodal learning (2008):

> *Experienced teachers recognize that the design of lessons must adapt to the expertise and prior knowledge of the learner, the complexity of the content, and interests of the learner. Experienced researchers recognize that the use of technology and multimedia, resources, and lessons can vary in the level of interactivity, modality, sequencing, pacing, guidance, prompts, and alignment to student interest, all of which influence the efficiency of the learning.*
>
> (p 8)

The report critiques obtuse views such as '*a picture is worth a thousand words*' and variations of the Confucius claim that '*I hear and I forget. I see and I remember. I do and I understand*'. In particular the report is critical of misinterpretations of Dale's Cone of Learning which was originally intended to be a visual means for identifying different modalities of learning rather than a hierarchy of effectiveness. What this means in practice is that '*doing is not always more efficient than seeing, and seeing is not always more effective than reading*' (p 24). For example, the report draws from a range of studies which suggest that interactive multimodal learning is more effective for learning higher order skills than basic skills, and non-interactive multimodal learning is better for learning basic skills rather than higher order skills.

Critical questions

> *Interactive multimodal learning includes collaborative learning, eg where a group of pupils discuss strategies when using a computer simulation. Non-interactive multimodal learning includes children watching a video or listening.*

» *Identify and evaluate occasions when you have used technology to assist learning which have involved (i) interactive and (ii) non-interactive learning.*

» *How might multimodal approaches to learning be used to help personalise children's learning experience?*

Multimodal: literacy

The national curriculum framework document (2013) specifically separates the school curriculum from the national curriculum (NC). It emphasises that the NC is part of the school curriculum and that schools are *'free to include other subjects or topics of their choice in planning and designing their own programme of education'* (p 5). When looking at the English programme of study there is no specific reference to digital content yet the concept of literacy itself has received a lot of attention in recent literature; for example, Walsh (2010, p 213) refers to *'visual literacy, new literacies, digital literacies, multimodality and multiliteracies'* when considering implications for classroom practice. This omission is potentially significant because of the more general trend for increased creation and consumption of digital content whether text messaging, tweeting, blogging, or any of the many other forms of Web 2.0. Research evidence also suggests different skills are needed for digital texts, eg *'navigation of screen-based texts frequently involves "radial browsing" which is quite different from left-to-right linear reading of print based texts'* (p 214).

Walsh (2010) provides a useful starting point for considering multimodal literacy in the context of the NC. Key learning areas are located within the encompassing context of different texts (print-based, digital, spoken and multimedia), mediums and modalities. For example, the key learning area *Talking and Listening* includes specific reference to *connecting* and *networking*; *Reading and Viewing* includes *browsing, searching, navigating* and *hyperlinking*; *Writing* includes *creating, designing* and *producing* (p 222).

The statutory content within the English NC includes retrieving, recording and presenting information from non-fiction. The non-statutory guidance identifies using the index and contents. This needs to be supplemented with approaches for information retrieval when reading digital texts. The focus on writing composition is similarly restricted in the English NC. The non-statutory guidance refers to headings, bullet points and underlining but doesn't give any attention to composing multimodal texts.

Critical questions

» *Refer to the English NC document and review the Spoken language, Reading and Writing non-statutory 'Notes and guidance'. Consider how you can accommodate the implications of multimodal literacy.*

» *Refer back to the* Time *(2012) magazine article. What place do e-books have in the primary classroom?*

Multimodal: primary science

Scientific understanding involves encountering and working with sensory data in multiple forms: feeling the force, seeing forces in action, representing forces in diagrammatic form and calculating force effects mathematically each contributes in its own way to the scientific understanding of the concept of force. Fitzgerald (2013) advises primary science teachers to make sure pupils experience and record scientific concepts in a variety of modalities, eg by doing investigations, discussing a video animation, recording using charts, interpreting and producing diagrams, drawing and talking about their ideas. And it's a short step from here to realise that you can use digital technology to facilitate access to multiple forms of data, eg using spreadsheet software, photography, video, audio recordings or one of the many apps available using mobile technology.

CASE STUDY

Year 5 evaporation lesson

Gillen et al (2008) focused on using affordances of the Interactive Whiteboard with a Key Stage 2 (Year 5) class to enable pupils to learn through different modalities. The multiple modalities are easily recognised and helped to make this a richer and more engaging learning experience for the pupils. The topic was introduced with a video illustrating evaporation. In the video the class teacher also talked to the class, including asking questions, as if being a virtual teacher – using visual and aural modalities and learning through interaction. In relation to other parts of the series of lessons still photos were taken as screenshots from the video and included along with captions to help with the verbal explanation. Some of the text, eg definition of evaporation, was emphasised using red text colour – making effective use of the visual modality. The lessons included whole-class discussions and during the discussion sections the teacher wrote annotations on screen. She also reinforced aspects of the topic through use of voice and gesture. The design of the screen enabled pupils to learn by actively rearranging items that had been located towards the bottom of the screen – learning through physical activity. The Interactive Whiteboard resource also supported continuity both within lessons and between lessons by allowing previous content to be revisited. In order to help the children understand the more abstract concept related to the topic the teacher created moving images of particles concealed by movable opaque rectangles. Children also learnt through role playing what it would be like to be particles in a solid, liquid and gas, eg standing close together with very limited movement when representing the solid. The teacher then revealed images by dragging the rectangles to one side.

Critical questions

» *Read through the science case study again and identify all the different modalities used by the teacher. How well do they fit into Murcia's* descriptive, experimental, mathematical, figurative *and* kinaesthetic *modalities?*

» *Numerous apps are readily available for the iPad. Choose a science topic and locate a suitable app for pupils to use when investigating the topic. Why have you chosen this particular app? What features make it fit for purpose?*

Digital technology and motivation

Yet a deeper understanding of the principles of reinforcement would not lead one to expect that frequent praise for short, easy tasks would create a desire for long, challenging ones or promote persistence in the face of failure.

(Dweck, 1986, p 1045)

Dweck's concepts of *performance goals* and *learning goals* are well known. The intrinsic motivation associated with the mastery-oriented learning goal is referred to as adaptive because it's characterised by persistence in the face of obstacles and initial failures. Pupils who are intrinsically motivated enjoy the challenge and can make a considerable effort when engaged in learning. Rather than blame themselves when confronted by difficulties for lacking ability or not being intelligent enough children with learning goals will re-evaluate their strategies, consider alternatives and redouble their efforts. On the other hand, extrinsic motivation that includes reward seeking, referred to by Dweck as maladaptive, is associated with higher levels of anxiety and avoidance in the face of potential failure. Children with performance motivation are more likely to choose easier, less challenging tasks in order to avoid failure, to blame failure on lack of ability and to give up easily.

Malone and Lepper (1987) produced a taxonomy of intrinsic motivations including individual motivations – curiosity, challenge, control and fantasy; and interpersonal motivations – competition, co-operation and recognition. The latter were believed to have greater longer term effects when endogenous to the learning task. For example, recognition – such as the award of a grade for work well done, was believed to be less effective than a more integral type of recognition – such as the pupil's work being used as an exemplar for other pupils. You can imagine the interest and engagement of a group of pupils working collaboratively to produce and publish a series of podcasts advertised as the school's radio programme. The recognition as parents and others respond to the content is likely to increase motivation even more. In fact, these types of authentic learning experience which involve manageable challenge and give pupils the autonomy to take control really are the gems of creative teaching. (Readers with a particular interest in motivation studies will find Malone and Lepper's taxonomy, originating in their study of digital games, and Ryan and Deci's (2000) review of intrinsic and extrinsic motivations useful starting points.)

At the start of the digital technology era in schools the technology itself was a particular source of interest. Even though the current news flow directs attention at impatient queues of consumers waiting for the latest product release from Apple or Sony, digital technology is now very much one of the tools of everyday life for the average person and child. The Interactive Whiteboard captivated attention when first introduced into schools but research suggests that children are not motivated specifically by technology in itself. However, for those children for whom Prensky's phrase *digital native* is appropriate, digital technology can be a very useful tool helping them to achieve their goals: learning in your native first language must surely be easier and experiencing success is itself motivating. The research of Granito and Chemobilsky (2012) with pupils aged 12–13 provides support for this view when concluding that *'technology has the potential to be a powerful educational tool for those that have an interest in it'* (p 19). However, they also discovered that *'greater achievement and knowledge retention*' (p 20) can occur without use of digital technology, particularly where pupils lack capability or interest in using digital technology.

Critical question

» *How as a teacher can you reconcile the point made by Granito and Chemobilsky with the legal requirement to teach all children digital literacy?*

Unpacking Malone and Lepper's taxonomy of intrinsic motivations will help you to recognise links to the digital technology environment within which learning occurs. A good starting point is Arnone et al (2011), who developed a theory of curiosity which includes links to interest and engagement. They refer to the broad encompassing environment as *learning modalities* which include ambient learning, cyberlearning and social networks. Personal, contextual and situational factors are regarded as having an impact within this broader digital environment. Table 3.1 identifies the proposed constituents of curiosity, interest and engagement. Essentially, where curiosity is aroused and followed up this can lead to different levels of interest and different types of engagement. For example, in relation to the cyberlearning modality which facilitates '*students learning by a variety of seamlessly integrated wireless technologies (e.g. radio, software, handhelds, social media) for learning anytime, anywhere*' (p 193), curiosity may be generated through an RSS feed that alerts the subscriber to new information on a topics of interest. This might happen within the formal school context or in the informal out-of-school context. The generated interest might then be developed into cognitive engagement supported by using a project planner, internet search engine, posting related messages on a social network site, contributing to a blog or wiki, as well as live discussion of the topic via Skype, etc. As a particular instance, consider the learning potential of establishing links to a school in a European (Key Stage 2) or non-European (Key Stage 1) country in relation to a national curriculum geography topic focused on place knowledge. Taking photos of the school and local area, producing videos, recording local interviews and pupils' perspectives on news events can all be published in blog format and connected to an RSS feed so that the partner school is alerted as new material is added.

Table 3.1 *Curiosity, interest and engagement*

Curiosity	Comprising trigger, reaction and resolution
Interest	A dimensional scale from the initial generated situational interest to well-developed individual interest
Engagement	Including a participation component where the activity was chosen by another, an affective component where engagement is due to the enjoyment of the activity and a cognitive component '*where the individual or group is fully and intrinsically committed to learning more about the phenomenon*' (Arnone et al, 2011, p 189)

Otta and Tavella (2010) focused on the link between student motivation and engagement when researching the use of digital mind games (puzzles and problem-solving software that require cognitive strategies) by pupils aged eight to ten years old. Their results reinforce the need to focus on transitory situational factors such as distractions and unexpected interruptions. However, the main contributing factor affecting engagement was found to be the success of the pupils when working on the learning tasks supported also by learner autonomy. Housand and Housand (2012) also emphasised the importance of challenge and autonomy as well as social and emotional needs when focusing on the role of technology for motivating gifted and talented pupils. They identified several potentially useful web sources such as the Johns Hopkins Center for Talented Youth (2013); the Khan Academy (2014), which contains thousands of video tutorials across a range of curriculum subjects suitable for gifted pupils in Key Stage 1/Key Stage 2; 3D GameLab (2014), supporting creation of personalised learning experiences; and the extensive store of free educational podcasts on iTunes. More generally you can use the internet to help gifted pupils have greater control and autonomy, enable connection with others with similar interests and to establish a sense of belonging and acceptance.

Critical questions

»   *Do an audit of children's interests in digital technology in your class or placement school. How might you respond to the different interests and abilities of the children when planning learning activities?*

»   *Focus on the range of digital technology that you have available in your school setting. How can you use this technology to arouse curiosity, ensure appropriately challenging learning tasks and give pupils control of the learning experience?*

Critical points

»   *Malone and Lepper's taxonomy of intrinsic motivation was introduced with a particular focus on the concept of curiosity. Take one of the other elements of the taxonomy (challenge, control, co-operation, collaboration, recognition) and investigate this further. For example, consider the various dimensions and connotations of challenge or control.*

»   *Specific examples of multimodal learning focused on literacy and science. Choose another curriculum area and refer to national curriculum statutory objectives and non-statutory guidance. Identify ways in which multimodal learning could help to enhance the quality of the school curriculum in this area.*

»   *In relation to personalisation, the chapter drew attention to Housand and Housand's article on the role of technology in gifted students' motivation. Consider the motivating role of technology in relation pupils with identified special educational needs or learning disabilities. For example, you might have experience of behaviourally challenging pupils so it would be useful to consider a role for digital technology in helping to improve interest and engagement.*

» *The use and educational value of digital games has been an undercurrent throughout the chapter. For example, Malone and Lepper's taxonomy originated from their study of computer games and Otta and Tavella's research evaluated pupils' responses to digital games requiring use of problem-solving strategies. Digital games can undoubtedly be highly motivating but as noted by Granito and Chernobilsky may not always result in effective learning. Take a more direct approach to considering the educational value of digital games by listing the affordances. A useful text is Marc Prensky's book* Digital Game Based Learning, *which contrasts the value of digital games in a range of contexts including industry, armed forces and various phases of school and other educational environments, eg flight simulators are a good training ground for pilots.*

Further reading and useful resources

Malone, T and Lepper, M (1987) Making Learning Fun: A Taxonomy of Intrinsic Motivations for Learning, in Snow, R and Farr, MJ (eds) *Aptitude, Learning and Instruction Vol 3: Conative and Affective Process Analyses.* Hillsdale, NJ, pp 223–53. [online] Available at: http://ocw.metu.edu.tr/mod/resource/view.php?id=1311 (accessed 31 October 2014).

Moreno, R and Mayer, R (2000) A Learner Centred Approach to Multimedia Explanations: Deriving Instructional Design Principles from Cognitive Theory. *Interactive Multimedia Electronic Journal of Computer-Enhanced Learning,* 2(2). [online] Available at: imej.wfu.edu/Articles/2000/2/05/index.asp (accessed 31 October 2014).

Prensky, M (2007) *Digital Game-Based Learning.* New York: Paragon House.

Ryan, R and Deci, L (2000) Intrinsic and Extrinsic Motivations: Classic Definitions and New Directions. *Contemporary Educational Psychology,* 25: 54–67. [online] Available at: mmrg.pbworks.com/f/Ryan,+Deci+00.pdf (accessed 31 October 2014).

References

3D GameLab (2014) [online] Available at: http://3dgamelab.com/personalized-quest-based-learning/ (accessed 31 October 2014).

Arnone, M, Small, R, Chauncey, S and McKenna, H (2011) Curiosity, Interest and Engagement in Technology-Pervasive Learning Environments: A New Research Agenda. *Education Tech Research Dev,* 59: 181–98. [online] Available at: www.marilynarnone.com/data/ETRDfulltext.pdf (accessed 31 October 2014).

Byron, T (2008) Safer Children in a Digital World. Department for Children, Schools and Families, and the Department for Culture, Media and Sport. [online] Available at: dera.ioe.ac.uk/7332/1/Final%20Report%20Bookmarked.pdf (accessed 31 October 2014).

Carr, N (2011) *Shallows: How the Internet is Changing the Way We Think, Read and Remember* [e-book]. Atlantic Books Ltd.

Cisco (2008) Multimodal Learning through Media: What the Research Says. Metiri Group. [online] Available at: www.cisco.com/web/strategy/docs/education/Multimodal-Learning-Through-Media.pdf (accessed 31 October 2014).

Department for Education (2013) *The National Curriculum in England: Framework Document.* [online] Available at: www.gov.uk/government/uploads/system/uploads/attachment_data/file/239033/PRIMARY_national_curriculum_-_Computing.pdf (accessed 31 October 2014).

Dweck, C (1986) Motivational Processes Affecting Learning. *American Psychologist,* 41(10): 1040–8. [online] Available at: psycnet.apa.org/psycinfo/1987-08696-001 (accessed 31 October 2014).

Fitzgerald, A (2013) *Learning and Teaching Primary Science.* New York: Cambridge University Press.

Gillen, J, Littleton, K, Twiner, A, Staarman, JK and Mercer, N (2008) Using the Interactive Whiteboard to Resource Continuity and Support Multimodal Teaching in a Primary Science Classroom. *Journal of Computer Assisted Learning,* 24: 348–58. [online] Available at: http://onlinelibrary.wiley.com/doi/10.1111/jca.2008.24.issue-4/issuetoc (accessed 31 October 2014).

Granito, M and Chemobilsky, E (2012) The Effect of Technology on a Student's Motivation and Knowledge Retention. *NERA Conference Proceedings,* Paper 17. [online] Available at: http://digitalcommons.uconn.edu/nera_2012/17 (accessed 31 October 2014).

Green, H, Facer, K, Rudd, T, Dillon, P and Humphreys, P (2005) *Personalisation and Digital Technologies.* Bristol: Futurelab.

Herrington, J and Kervin, L (2007) Authentic Learning Supported by Technology: 10 Suggestions and Cases of Integration in Classrooms. *Research Online.* [online] Available at: ro.uow.edu.au/cgi/viewcontent.cgi?article=1027&context=edupapers (accessed 31 October 2014).

Housand, B and Housand, A (2012) The Role of Technology in Gifted Students' Motivation. *Psychology in the Schools,* 49(7): 706–15. [online] Available at: http://onlinelibrary.wiley.com/doi/10.1002/pits.21629/full (accessed 31 October 2014).

Jabr, F (2013) Why the Brain Prefers Paper. *Scientific American,* 309(5): 48–53. [online] Available at: www.nature.com/scientificamerican/journal/v309/n5/full/scientificamerican1113-48.html (accessed 31 October 2014).

Johns Hopkins Center for Talented Youth (2013) [online] Available at: http://cty.jhu.edu/ctyonline (accessed 31 October 2014).

Jones, J (2013) How Does Electronic Reading Affect Comprehension? [online] Available at: dmlcentral.net/blog/john-jones/how-does-electronic-reading-affect-comprehension (accessed 31 October 2014).

Jones, J (2014) Study Proves Why We Need Digital Literacy Education. [online] Available at: dmlcentral.net/blog/john-jones/study-proves-why-we-need-digital-literacy-education (accessed 31 October 2014).

Khan Academy (2014) [online] Available at: www.khanacademy.org/ (accessed 31 October 2014).

Kress, G (2010) *Multimodality: A Social Semiotic Approach to Contemporary Communication.* London: Routledge.

Malone, T and Lepper, M (1987) Making Learning Fun: A Taxonomy of Intrinsic Motivations for Learning. In Snow, R and Farr, MJ (eds) *Aptitude, Learning and Instruction Vol 3: Conative and Affective Process Analyses.* Hillsdale, NJ. pp 223–53. [online] Available at: http://ocw.metu.edu.tr/mod/resource/view.php?id=1311 (accessed 31 October 2014).

McFarlane, A (1997) *Information Technology and Authentic Learning.* London: Routledge.

Miller, M (2009) What the Science of Cognition Tells Us about Instructional Technology. *Change: The Magazine of Higher Learning*, 41(2): 16–17. [online] Available at: dx.doi.org/10.3200/CHNG.41.2.16-17 (accessed 31 October 2014).

Moreno, R and Mayer, R (2000) A Learner Centred Approach to Multimedia Explanations: Deriving Instructional Design Principles from Cognitive Theory. *Interactive Multimedia Electronic Journal of Computer-Enhanced Learning*, 2(2). [online] Available at: imej.wfu.edu/Articles/2000/2/05/index.asp (accessed 31 October 2014).

Murcia, K (2010) Multi-Modal Representations in Primary Science: What's Offered by Interactive Whiteboard Technology. *Teaching Science*, 56(1): 23–9. [online] Available at: caitlan-space. wikispaces.com/file/view/What+is+Offered+.pdf (accessed 18 August 2014).

NAACE (2001) Key Characteristics of Good Quality Teaching and Learning with ICT: A Discussion Document. [online] Available at: revolution.caret.cam.ac.uk/pdfs/bectaadvice.pdf (accessed 31 October 2014).

Otta, M and Tavella, M (2010) Motivation and Engagement in Computer-Based Learning Tasks: Investigating Key Contributing Factors. *World Journal on Educational Technology*, 2(1): 1–15. [online] Available at: www.world-education-center.org/index.php/wjet/article/view/57/pdf_12 (accessed 31 October 2014).

Papert, S (1998) [online] Available at: www.papert.org/articles/Childpower.html (accessed 31 October 2014).

Plowden Report (1967) Children and Their Primary Schools. [online] Available at: www.educationeng-land.org.uk/documents/plowden/plowden1967-1.html (accessed 31 October 2014).

Prensky, M (2007) *Digital Game-Based Learning*. New York: Paragon House.

Ryan, R and Deci, L (2000) Intrinsic and Extrinsic Motivations: Classic Definitions and New Directions. *Contemporary Educational Psychology*, 25: 54–67. [online] Available at: mmrg.pbworks.com/f/Ryan,+Deci+00.pdf (accessed 31 October 2014).

Sky News (2009) Video War Games Boost 'Working Memory'. [online] Available at: news.sky.com/story/723027/video-war-games-boost-working-memory (accessed 31 October 2014).

StateUniversity.com (2014) Progressive Education – Philosophical Foundations, Pedagogical Progressivism, Administrative Progressivism, Life-Adjustment Progressivism. [online] Available at: education.stateuniversity.com/pages/2336/Progressive-Education.html (accessed 31 October 2014).

Time (2012) Do e-Books Make it Harder to Remember What You Just Read? [online] Available at: healthland.time.com/2012/03/14/do-e-books-impair-memory/ (accessed 31 October 2014).

Walsh, M (2010) Multimodal Literacy: What Does it Mean for Classroom Practice? *Australian Journal of Language and Literacy*, 33(3): 211–39. [online] Available at: www.alea.edu.au/documents/item/63 (accessed 31 October 2014).

4 Information literacy for teachers and learners

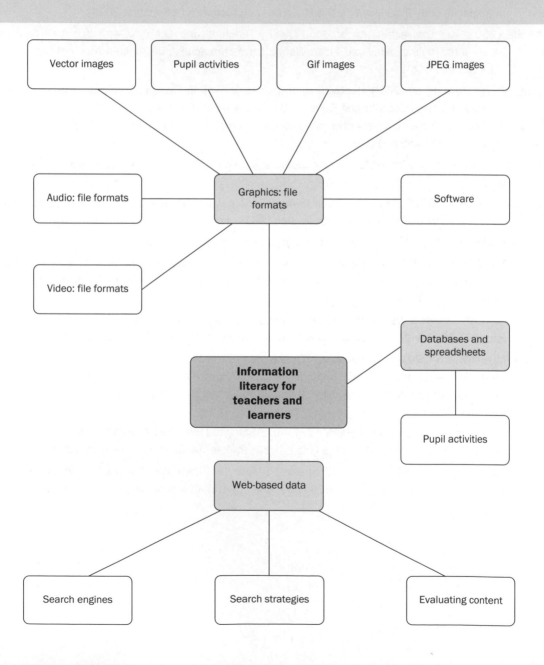

Introduction: data, information and knowledge

Simply stated, the raw data of experience becomes meaningful when transformed into *information* through being placed in a context. For example, a string of numbers such as 116, 137, 127, 128, 129, 125, could be regarded as data though without the context it's just a string of numbers. Once you identify the numbers as measurements of the heights of ten-year-old boys in your class the data is starting to be informative. However, for information to lead to knowledge there needs to be enough information for decisions to be made. If your class were doing a topic on healthy lifestyle and diet for example you would also need information about weight (though bear in mind that topics including personal information need to be handled sensitively). The pupils could then use the National Health Service (NHS) statistics for the body mass index (BMI) to help determine healthy weight. In other words when the NHS screening at age ten identifies a boy whose height is 129cms but weight is 31.5kg then action to reduce weight would be advised. The BBC Bitesize website provides a straightforward overview of the connection between data, information and knowledge (www.bbc.co.uk/schools/gcsebitesize/ict/).

$$\text{Data} \longrightarrow \text{Information} \longrightarrow \text{Knowledge}$$

Of course measurements of length and weight are different forms of data and data takes many forms. There are also numerous tools and approaches that you can use with your pupils for working with and converting data into knowledge. The national curriculum for computing in Key Stages 1 and 2 recognises this and focuses directly on teaching children to work with data in a range of digital formats using a range of digital devices: at Key Stage 1, '*organise, store, manipulate and retrieve data in a range of digital formats*', and at Key Stage 2, '*select, use and combine a variety of software (including internet services) on a range of digital devices to accomplish given goals, including collecting, analysing, evaluating and presenting data and information*' (DFE, 2013).

Databases and spreadsheets

Types of data are brought into sharp focus when working with databases and spreadsheets. Both databases and spreadsheets store different types of data as different field types which constrain ways of working with the data. Typical field types are number, currency, date, time and text, though may also include yes/no, images, hyperlinks and calculated fields as well as *key words* or *look up* fields amongst others. The field type is usually associated with different properties such as *field size*, *format* and *validation rule* which also delimit ways of working with the data. This added precision is useful for avoiding errors when working with data.

Continuing with the healthy lifestyle example, you could use a flat file database to investigate health and development of children. When creating the database you would need to include a record for each individual child (Figure 4.1) which contains details such as name, sex, age, weight, height, etc. The *First name* and *Surname* fields, where the individual child's name is entered, would need to be text fields to make sure only text was entered. The *Sex* field could usefully be set as a key words field so that only *boy* or *girl* can be entered to avoid spelling mistakes and variations such as *By* or *B* which would prevent some of the data being found when searching. If the *Age* field type is then set to *number* and a *validation rule* created [Age is <12] then when inputting pupils' ages the only data accepted by the database would be numbers less than 12 and this would also help to reduce possible typing errors. A further advantage of selecting an appropriate field type occurs when searching the data: setting the *Age* to a numerical field type allows searching using numerical operators, eg >8 and <11 would find all children older than 8 but younger than 11. Search strategies are considered in detail later in the chapter.

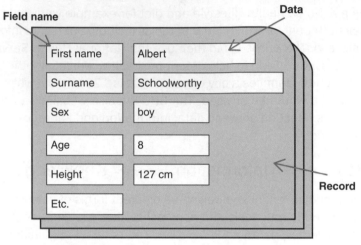

Figure 4.1 *Record, field names and data*

Pupil activities

The national curriculum for computing includes teaching children to use a variety of software to accomplish a learning task.

- Database software intended for primary schools such as the *RM Softease Database*, Black Cat's *Information Workshop 2000* and Logotron's *Junior Viewpoint* allows the pupils to include information from a range of sources. For example, they can use a digital camera to take photos of themselves or their pets and store these in an *image field*.

- The archive for *teachers.tv* videos includes a creative and enterprising approach to Key Stage 2 personal, social and health education (PSHE) – related to personal finance education – in which the pupils take responsibility for planning and managing a school disco (www.creativeeducation.co.uk/videos/watch-video.aspx?id=2999). Projects of this sort are full of opportunities for making authentic use of a range of software and digital devices. In the school disco project pupils used a spreadsheet to calculate projected costs and profits as well as desktop publishing software to design fliers advertising the disco. The event itself can also be videoed used for promotional purposes on the school website.

- Another authentic use for a database would be for book reviews. Children could review books and add the reviews to a flat file database and this could also become the basis for a class library system. NB A branching database would also be useful for choosing books.

Critical questions

» *Identify and evaluate the database and spreadsheet software being used in your context.*

» *Plan a cross-curricula project that enables the pupils in your class to make authentic use of a database.*

Graphics: file formats

The following sections help you to understand the different graphics file formats, uses and software. The main categories of graphics images are *raster* (commonly referred to as bit-map images) and *vector* graphics.

JPEG images

Rasterised images are made up of pixels which are very small coloured squares. Each individual square of colour takes up memory in the computer so bitmap images can be very large files and are not a suitable format for website images or when sending email attachments. When editing a bitmap image changes are made to each pixel. An extreme close up of a bitmap image shows jagged tooth edges because of the way the small squares of colour are positioned (see Figure 4.2).

The pixels are so tiny that the human eye doesn't notice if some of the pixels are removed. Compressing images by removing unnecessary pixels is good news for the file size. A very common file type for images is *jpg* or *jpeg* (developed by the Joint Photographic Expert Group) which uses *lossy* compression (ie there is a loss of image quality through removal of some of the pixels). Images that may run into several megabytes as a bitmap will only be a few hundred kilobytes as a JPEG image. This means they download very quickly and are ideal when sending as an email attachment or for a webpage.

You should therefore teach your pupils to save graphics files as jpg or jpeg when the learning outcomes for the topic include sending emails with attachments or creating a webpage.

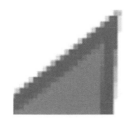

Figure 4.2 *Bitmap image*

GIF images

An alternative type of bitmap image is the *GIF* image (Graphics Interchange Format). This uses a maximum of 256 colours and the image compression occurs by reducing the number of colours (lossless) rather than by reducing the number of pixels (lossy). Consequently the GIF file format is not suitable for photographic images. However, the GIF format does allow for creating transparent images (Figure 4.3), which is not possible with the jpg/jpeg format, and is also useful for animated images. GIF is an ideal format for an animated logo that has less than 256 colours.

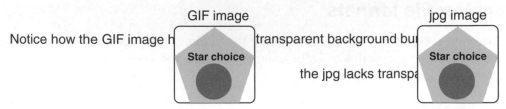

Figure 4.3 *Notice how the text is concealed by the jpg image*

Pupil activities

The national curriculum for computing includes teaching children to use a variety of software to accomplish a learning task.

*   In a design and technology project pupils could use software such as *2D Primary* (www.techsoft.co.uk/products/software/2D_Primary.asp) to create a net view of their product and then use graphics software such as Logotron's *Revelation Natural Art* (www.r-e-m.co.uk/logo/?Titleno=25343) to create a logo for the product they design. Using the transparency afforded by the GIF format would allow just the logo itself to be visible. As part of the design process pupils could also use a digital camera to take photos during the making process and use these photos for ongoing evaluation and review.

Vector images

Vector based graphics are calculated by the software and are not based on pixels. This means that zooming in to a high magnification level does not result in jagged edges (Figure 4.4).

Figure 4.4 *Vector images*

Vector images are typically edited by adding anchor points using the pen tool; this can be quite tricky to get used to when using advanced graphics software such as *Adobe Illustrator* but useful for drawing cartoons and producing fashion designs. File sizes are small because images are based on calculations rather than pixels. Note that when using the Shapes in *MSWord 2010* it's possible to edit the shapes. (Increase the zoom level and check that the shapes drawn in *MSWord* are vector images rather than bitmap images.)

Audio: file formats

When digital technology is used to record sound, the sound has first of all to be transformed into binary data. The computer or other digital device uses a *codec* to code and decode the audio data so that it can be saved as a file format. As with graphics file formats, audio may be saved using *lossless* or *lossy* compression.

*   The most well-known lossless file type is the *wav* file (for Windows PC) and *aiff* file (for Apple Mac). Because no data is removed wav and aiff the files are high quality audio but have a very large file size.

*   The most well know lossy file type is the *MP3* file, which can also be excellent quality to the human ear but also has a much smaller file size.

Sometimes it's necessary to install a particular codec before being able to save the audio in your preferred file type. For example, software such as *Audacity*, which is useful for creating podcasts, requires you to install a codec before you can save files in the MP3 format (see Chapter 6 for more details on this).

Video: file formats

The good news if you are using the latest *Windows Live Movie Maker 12* is that this video editing software supports wav, aiff and MP3 audio formats (so no need to install any codecs); it also allows you to save your video files as wmv or mpeg-4/h.264.

As with audio files different software may support different file types and file size, quality and purpose will help you decide which file type to choose.

*   A file format such as avi uses a lossless codec and produces excellent quality but very large file sizes. This is a good format for doing high quality video editing but not suitable for sending as an email attachment or for uploading to a web page.

*   A file format such as wmv uses lossy compression which reduces the quality of the video but also has a much smaller file size. This format can also be played using Windows Media Player which means anyone with a PC can watch your video. However, if you have an Apple Mac computer you'll need to download a plugin or a multi-format media player such as VLC media player (vlc-media-player.en.softonic. com/).

*   The mov file format uses the Apple Quick Time video player which is playable on both Windows and Apple Mac computers.

- The Adobe Flash video format *swf* was designed to allow video to be streamed from the internet but Flash video can't be viewed on all devices, eg it's not supported by the iPhone.

Software

The range of graphics software specifically intended for use in primary schools includes painting programs such as 2Simple's *2paint a picture*, *Revelation Natural Art*, *Paint.NET*, *Paint Shop Pro*. These programs have a range of features worth exploring, eg *Paint Shop Pro* allows pupils to work with layers and *2paint a picture* introduces a range of artistic effects and styles. It's also worth noting that software such as *Revelation Natural Art* can be set for different age groups and levels. Programs such as the free version of Google's *Sketchup* and *2D Primary* are object oriented vector based graphics programs that support design type activities. The well-known *iMovie* and *Windows Movie Maker Live* are easy to use and include basic editing features. For more able upper Key Stage 2 children who already have some experience of video editing *Adobe Premiere Elements* would allow you introduce a wider range of editing features. For more on using software to create content see Chapter 5.

Critical questions

» *You have been introduced to a few of the many file formats for graphics, audio and video that are in common use. Research the characteristics of file formats such as png, tiff, midi, mpeg-4 and h.264.*

» *Plan a cross-curricular project for a Key Stage 2 class which involves using* Sketchup *as well as a painting program. How can you address the national curriculum for computing learning objectives in this project?*

Web-based data

The national curriculum requires that pupils are taught to:

> Use search technologies effectively, appreciate how results are selected and ranked, and be discerning in evaluating digital content.

> (NC, 2013 p 189)

Search engines

The national curriculum uses the plural *search technologies* and if you browse the internet for a few minutes you'll rapidly locate an impressive array of search engines which provide more or less access to both the surface web and deep or invisible and dark web. The surface web is essentially all the easily located websites that most browsers can access whereas the invisible web includes content held in password protected databases, dynamically registered content and content not registered with search engines. Devine and Egger-Sider (2009), in their book *Going Beyond Google*, provide a comprehensive overview of using the invisible web in learning and teaching; and the 21st Century Information Fluency

Project (21CIF) (21cif.com/tutorials/challenge/) includes a series of tutorials related to the invisible web intended for primary school pupils. Statistics suggest the deep web is at least 500 times the size of the surface web; academic study can be greatly enhanced by accessing database content through, eg Academic Search Premiere or Summon. Some search engines such as www.scholar.google.co.uk are a half-way house.

You'll find it useful to categorise search engines by the way they operate. Different search engines find and store data in different ways so it's useful to consider a range of types including directories, visual and semantic search engines.

Subject directories

These support pupils learning how to categorise information. They work by starting with a more general category which is then gradually refined by selecting more specific categories until the question prompting the search is answered.

Numerous subject directories designed for children are easily accessed on the internet, including:

*   www.kidsclick.org An example search for information on ancient Rome would begin by selecting the category Geography/History followed by World history and then Rome (Ancient). The resulting list of websites are helpfully categorized using the subheadings Illustrations and Reading level together with a few sentences describing the website.

*   www.kidsites.org This directory includes sections for Toddlers, Primary, Teachers, Preschoolers, Family & Parenting and Shopping Online.

*   www.ipl.org This is the Internet Public Library which includes a For Kids section as well as resources for parents and teachers.

*   www.childrenslibrary.org This is a combination of category search and visual search. For example, Books by Country are accessed by turning an image of the globe and pointing with the mouse. The children's books in the Read books section are searched using colourful icons, eg the short books icon shows a thinner book than the long books icon, fairy tales are represented by an Aladdin's lamp icon; books for 3–5-year-olds are represented by the silhouette of a toddler whereas the 10–13 category is depicted by the silhouette of an older child running.

Visual search engines

These include search engines that show images of the website rather than textual summaries as indicators of the content. Visual search engines also may show network views indicating relevance as well as links between the results of the search. This approach to searching can be useful if you have pupils with a visual learning style, for younger children and also for those with dyslexia.

Joho and Jose (2005) note that when search results are represented on the page in multiple formats rather than simply visual images or text this extends the range of contexts for determining relevance and provides searchers with more control. However, they also note that the greater complexity of a search results page containing multiple formats can require more cognitive effort. They emphasise the importance of context when explaining that snippets of text from a website are less effective as a search result than sentences contextualised by the search query. They also focus on how use of thumbnail images can speed up the searcher's assessment of relevance but can also lead to false judgments.

- http://camfindapp.com/ CamFind is a great way to search without having to type anything. Simply point the camera eg a screen cam attached to the computer and, hey presto, the image is analysed and results are displayed in the browser.

- http://redz.com RedZ returns search results as a carousel of images of web pages, images or videos. It also allows the user to switch to a visual matrix. The simple format and friendly red striped cuddly toy increase the appeal for use by children.

- http://oskope.com/ This visual search engine is useful for searching through YouTube videos and Flickr images though it also includes Amazon and eBay.

- www.touchgraph.com/seo This approach to searching displays the results as a clickable map showing the connections between the located websites. Related searches, search results and top domains are also included in text format on the left of the screen (Figure 4.5). Claims made by TouchGraph SEO include being able to visualise connections and being able to '*explore clusters of similar websites*'. This search engine also fits the *poly-representation* model advocated by Joho and Jose (2005), although it incorporates icons rather than thumbnail images.

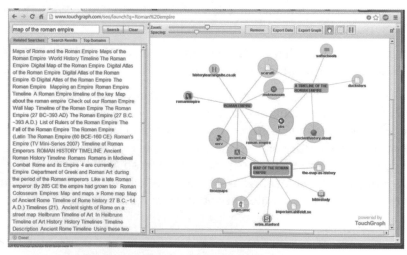

Figure 4.5 *Screenshot showing interconnected search results using touchgraph.com/seo*

Semantic search engines

Search engines typically work by using an algorithm to determine the result of the search including the order for displaying the results (see the section on Google for more on this). Semantic search engines, on the other hand, search using the meaning of the search terms.

One consequence of this is that results may be grouped according to the different connotations of the search term. For example, searching for *apple* may result in websites grouped into *apple fruit* meanings separated from the *Apple technology* meanings separated from the *Big Apple* meanings, etc. Semantic search engines are essentially part of the semantic web, also referred to as Web 3.0 (Devine and Egger-Sider, 2009). As the semantic web develops, more complex searches at the click of a button will become possible. Web 3.0 suggests a more intelligent search engine that also learns and adapts to the searcher's search needs. An interesting and perhaps disturbing perspective on the semantic web is presented by Patrick Tucker (2014) in his book *The Naked Future – What Happens in a World that Anticipates Your Every Move?* Even though the semantic web is still in its infancy some of the semantic web search engines may still be useful:

- www.sensebot.net This search engine provides brief meaning based set of results, ie not quoted snippets of text from the websites but text related to the interpreted meaning of the search phrase. The results page also includes a semantic cloud which is a collection of hyperlinked words related to the original search phrase. Similar to wordle (www.wordle.net/) the larger the font size the more relevant the connection. For example, when searching for Roman empire the semantic cloud comprised 27 hyperlinked words (Rome, Roman and empire were very large text; government, history, ancient, Augustus, etc were medium size; words such as power, influence, city and battle were small font size). The results page also included six different websites and brief comments related to the search term.

- Potential value in the primary school: although the search results page is text only this can be seen as reducing distractions and cognitive load. The typically small number of visible results and the potential value of the sematic cloud help make the results more accessible.

- duckduckgo.com/ This search engine interprets and categorises connotations of the search term where there is any ambiguity. It helpfully provides a grid of thumbnails of the different meanings as well as the list of results of the search, including images and videos. For example, searching for fairy returns six categories of meanings: Top, Tradition and Mythology, Plants and Animals, Popular Culture, Other, See Also.

- kngine.com/ The results page shows just a few answers to the search query so the impression is simplicity. The answer is sometimes something like, 'I'm not sure about the answer but try this page'. It's also possible to show a short list of related web link results. This enhances the appeal of Kngine but the text preview descriptions are very brief and there are also links to Twitter, Facebook, Google+ and other menu items that could be potential distractions.

Vertical search engines

Search engines such as www.Google.com and uk.search.yahoo.com/, sometimes referred to as horizontal search engines, are generic. More specialised searches may be better supported by using a vertical search engine. Google itself has a range of vertical search engines, eg Google Maps, Google Image Search and YouTube. Social media websites such as www.teachertube.com/ and www.flickr.com/ can be really useful, eg searching Flickr for *Worcester*

UK floods returns numerous photos with a Creative Commons copyright. Retail companies also include search engines within their websites, eg Blackwell Bookshop allows searching and ordering books online. Online newspapers allow searching for news items and may be more useful than generic search engines.

Google

A simple way of understanding how a search engine works is to analyse the process into three parts: crawl, index and rank. This essentially amounts to the search engine becoming aware of the content of web pages, keeping a record (index) and then using algorithms to determine the order of displayed results (rank) www.youtube.com/watch?v=KyCYyoGusqs.

There are more than a trillion pages on the world wide web, so first of all the search engine *crawls* its way through all the web pages on the internet, following the links from page to page. Google's approach is to crawl the entire web and refresh the indexed data on a daily basis but to refresh supplemental pages, the long tail of the web, less frequently. Indexing involves using a system to record the data matched to search terms. Whereas approaches to ranking search results include counting the number of times a search term appears in the text of the website, Google's approach includes identifying the number of times a web page has been linked to by other web pages. This page ranking approach recognises that webpages that are linked to by other websites have potentially greater perceived value and so appear closer to the top of the list of search results. The final order is also affected by website creators' use of key words added to the metadata when creating the web page and by purchase of Google AdWords.

Search strategies

A useful way of thinking about search strategies is by focusing on the purpose of the search, use of search terms, search operators and search tactics.

Search purpose

You will need to teach the pupils the appropriate strategy for the purpose. For example, finding the answer to a straightforward specific fact based question will require a different strategy compared to a more open-ended exploratory investigation of a topic. A directory may actually be more effective when the purpose is to browse a general area of interest whereas a search engine is more appropriate when looking for specific information. Making sure your pupils are clear about the purpose, whether it's finding a video, an image, reliable viewpoints on a topic, quantitative data or up-to-date news, will help focus attention and improve their chances of success.

Search terms

Teaching pupils to use a thesaurus will help them generate alternative search terms (the-saurus.com/). It's also worth considering the potential impact of different spellings, eg UK or USA. You also need to explain that high information content words and subject specific words (the jargon) are a far better choice than more common words as this will reduce the number of irrelevant results. In fact many common words such as *the, a, but, have, in, and* and *not* (referred to as *stop* words) are ignored altogether by search engines; though some upper case words such as *AND* and *NOT* are logical operators that are used when constructing search queries (see next section). And just to complicate things, some web browsers give different results depending on the order of the search terms. Placing search terms within inverted commas makes sure the search terms are used precisely as written, eg *'fall of roman empire'* will give a different result to *'empire roman fall of'*.

Search operators

Operators are used to build queries and queries help make the search more precise:

> *AND (or +) This can be useful for ensuring that a search term is included in the results, eg a search for* worcester *AND* uk *would separate the UK Worcester from the Worcester in Massachusetts.*

> *NOT (or -) This can also be useful for reducing the number of results by omitting irrelevant details, eg a search for* blackberry NOT device NOT phone.

A point worth noting is that different search engines use different hidden operators. For example, www.google.com uses AND as the default operator whereas uk.search.yahoo.com uses OR as the default operator: consequently when using a series of keywords such as *blackberry guava fruit mountain phone* Google will only find websites that contain each of these key words but Yahoo will find websites that contain any of these keywords. The search help page for the search engine being used will give specific details of more advanced operators such as allintitle: site: link: and info: Google's Web Search Support can be accessed from support.google.com/ (NB This also includes details of using Safe Search to avoid adult content in the search results).

Search tactics

Xia and Joo (2010) provide an extensive review of the literature focusing on strategies people use when searching the internet. Their own approach, based on 13 search tactics, identifies eight types of strategy grouped into five categories. The most frequent types of search strategy are what they refer to as *Iterative result evaluation, Iterative exploration* and *Query initiation* (if you are looking for a range of search strategies Xia and Joo would be useful further reading).

Of course there may not be any one ideal approach to ensure success when searching but a useful resource for Key Stage 2 primary pupils has been developed by the 21st Century Information Fluency Project (21CIF) 21cif.com/tutorials/challenge/. This provides a series of search challenges and well-designed tutorials at six levels. These are linked to specific competencies based on the International Society for Technology in Education (ISTE) standards but they also share common ground with the UK national curriculum for computing (www.iste.org/home). Specific learning objectives relate to use of search strategy, use of keywords, use of *nyms* (synonym, hyponym and hypernym), browsing hyperlinks, use of databases, use of operators, using a subject directory, focus on investigative searching and defining the search question.

Critical questions

» *Subject directories function in a similar way to branching databases so it could be useful to plan a series of lessons involving both. How might you do this? Would it be better to start by teaching the pupils to use a subject directory and then move on to create a branching database or vice versa?*

» *Try out and evaluate a range of search engines. Which are more suited to Key Stage 1 and which would be better for Key Stage 2?*

Evaluating content

Richardson and McBryde-Wilding (2009) refer to three different sets of criteria for evaluating information: the generic '*provenance, access, currency, content and intended audience*'; and criteria specifically for websites: '*currency, authority, reliability, purpose, coverage, style and functionality*' (from the Cornell University Library); '*ownership, authority, currency, quality of content and intended audience*' (from Rumsey, 2004). The criteria are not presented as a rigid tick-box type approach but rather as suggestions for kick-starting the evaluation process. They urge students to develop their own criteria and specific evaluation questions as they become more experienced at evaluating information. Benjes-Small et al (2013) develop this emphasis on flexibility by adopting a constructivist approach to evaluating websites where students are supported in developing their own criteria. Strict application of evaluation frameworks can lead to ticking boxes rather than careful analysis and evaluation. For example, a dot com website, although being commercially oriented, may still be useful and shouldn't be automatically discarded. Similarly, if a website source hasn't been updated for an extended period it shouldn't be automatically discarded for lack of currency. Harris (2013) reinforces this need for interpretation when describing source evaluation as an art and expresses the view that '*there is no single perfect indicator of reliability, truthfulness, or value. Instead, you must make an inference from a collection of clues or indicators, based on the use you plan to make of your source*'.

Website evaluation in the primary school

Richardson and McBryde-Wilding (2009) begin by focusing on the concept of critical thinking. Although the question of whether the internet is unregulated or not is debatable it is a recognisably open environment where, for practical purposes, anything goes. Talking about the internet and the content with your class will help to raise awareness of the uncertainty of the world wide web and the potential unreliability of first impressions.

Benjes-Small et al (2013) approached developing evaluation skills by focusing on who, what, when, where and why. The meanings of these 5Ws are readily interpretable in relation to the evaluation frameworks referred to above, eg who would be a good author and publisher of the website? How accurate is the content? Are there any typographical errors in the content? Where – would the website be better as a dot com, dot org, dot edu, etc? When was the content last modified? The approach described by Benjes-Small et al began with small groups of students being given a spoof website to evaluate (eg bigredhair.com/boilerplate/) and asked to give five reasons demonstrating that the website lacked credibility. This was followed by a whole-class discussion and general criteria recorded on the whiteboard using the 5Ws as prompts. This was followed by the students being assigned a topic and challenged to think up *gold standard* criteria and evaluation questions for websites related to their topic. In the final activity the task was a competition for each group to find a website that matched the gold standard for their topic.

Whereas this approach avoids ticking boxes it can be quite challenging to recognise spoof websites such as Boilerplate and Tree Octopus (zapatopi.net/treeoctopus/) as they are so well developed and may require a high standard of reading ability. However, the 21st Century Information Fluency Project includes tutorials and challenges in the *Information Forensics* section (21cif.com/) useful for developing evaluation skills.

Critical question

» *Try some of the website evaluation activities available on the 21st Century Fluency Project website. Consider the experience and ability of the children in your class and devise your own evaluation challenges.*

Critical points

» *Andretta (2005) focuses on reservations about use of the term* literacy *and identifies alternatives such as* 'information skills, information handling, information fluency' *(p 17).*

» *Haythornewaite and Andrews (2011) prefer the phrase* discourse *rather than* literacy *(p 70), suggesting that literacy is an overused term. The older concept of* bibliographic instruction *also helps to draw attention to the non-digital world of information.*

» *This chapter has focused directly on digital data and information, including file formats, types of search engine search and evaluation strategies in the digital context. Is* information literacy *the best phrase to use or would* digital information literacy *or even* digital information discourse *be a better choice?*

Further reading and useful resources

Different types of database include flat file, branching and relational: www.igcseict.info/theory/5/dbtypes/.

You can find out more about image, audio and video file types from the following web sources:

• JPG versus GIF for web images: users.wfu.edu/matthews/misc/jpg_vs_gif/JpgVsGif.html.

• Choosing a digital audio format: www.jiscdigitalmedia.ac.uk/guide/choosing-a-digital-audio-file-format.

• Movie Maker 12 – your very own movie studio: http://windows.microsoft.com/en-gb/windows-live/movie-maker.

The following book is useful as a general introduction to information skills:

- Richardson, L and McBryde-Wilding, H (2009) *Information Skills for Education Students.* Exeter: Learning Matters.

Find out more about search strategies by reading:

- Xia, I and Joo, S (2010) Tales from the Field: Search Strategies Applied in Web Searching. *Future Internet,* 2: 259–81. [online] Available at: www.mdpi.com/1999-5903/2/3/259 (accessed 31 October 2014).

You can search for resources that have a Creative Commons licence using the Creative Commons website:

- search.creativecommons.org/.

See how the internet is changing by reading the following news item:

- Yahoo news (2012) How the Internet Will Get New Domain Name Suffixes. [online] Available at: news.yahoo.com/internet-domain-name-suffixes-070330403--finance.html (accessed 31 October 2014).

References

Andretta, S (2005) *Information Literacy: A Practitioner's Guide.* Oxford: Chandos Publishing Ltd.

Benjes-Small, C, Archer, A, Tucker, K, Vassady, L and Resor, J (2013) Teaching Web Evaluation. *Communication in Information Literacy,* 7(1): 39–49.

Department for Education (2013) *The National Curriculum in England: Framework Document.* [online] Available at: www.gov.uk/government/uploads/system/uploads/attachment_data/file/239033/PRIMARY_national_curriculum_-_Computing.pdf (accessed 31 October 2014).

Devine, J and Egger-Sider, F (2009) *Going Beyond Google.* London: Facet Publishing.

Harris, R (2013) Evaluating Internet Research Sources. [online] Available at: www.virtualsalt.com/evalu8it.htm (accessed 31 October 2014).

Haythornewaite, C and Andrews, R (2011) *E-learning Theory & Practice.* London: Sage.

Joho, H and Jose, J (2005) Effectiveness of Additional Representations for the Search Result Presentation on the Web. [online] Available at: www.dcs.gla.ac.uk/~hideo/pub/ipm07/ipm07.pdf (accessed 31 October 2014).

NC (2013) National Curriculum. [online] Available at: www.gov.uk/government/uploads/system/uploads/attachment_data/file/210969/NC_framework_document_-_FINAL.pdf (accessed 31 October 2014).

Richardson, L and McBryde-Wilding, H (2009) *Information Skills for Education Students.* Exeter: Learning Matters

Tucker, P (2014) *The Naked Future.* New York: Penguin.

Xia, I and Joo, S (2010) Tales from the Field: Search Strategies Applied in Web Searching. *Future Internet,* 2: 259–81. [online] Available at: www.mdpi.com/1999-5903/2/3/259 (accessed 31 October 2014).

5 Creating content

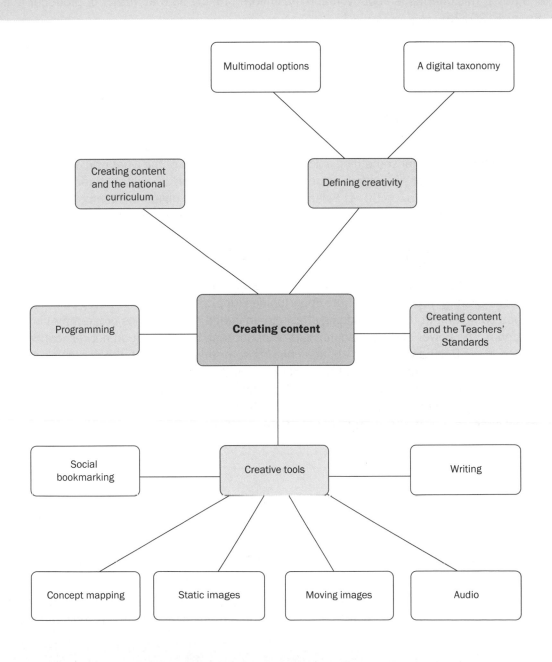

Introduction

Creativity might not have been the first element that sprung to mind when you started thinking about digital literacy, but hopefully the book so far has convinced you that in fact creativity is a crucial component. Children will be creating digital artefacts to convey to you what they know, understand and can do both individually and/or collaboratively. As a teacher you want to introduce them to the approaches and tools that are going to empower them to express themselves and convey their capabilities, knowledge and understanding in the most enabling form available. Returning to the *consumer* or *author* discussion raised in Chapter 1, this chapter is about you and the children taking on that *author* or producer role (Resnick, 2012a).

By creating content the children are producing a manifestation of their thinking for others to witness or interact with. Resnick phrased this as an '*external representation of the ideas in your head*' (2012b, pp 50–1). This step is key in terms of metacognition for children (helping them to recognise and understand their thinking processes) as it enables them '*to play*' with their '*ideas and gain a better understanding of the possibilities and limitations of*' their ideas; including '*what would happen if…?*' (Resnick, 2012b, pp 50–1).

Digital technologies offer something uniquely powerful in terms of the *what would happen if …* component; and Belshaw picked up on this in his discussion of digital literacy and *confidence* (Resnick, 2012b, pp 50–1; Belshaw, 2011, p 10). The digital environment is low-risk for experimentation, you can try something and click undo if you don't like it, save multiple versions, and mix media in a click. This can be very appealing to those children fearful of making mistakes, not wanting to try things. In our experience this provisionality affordance is very liberating for some children; sometimes, simply because a task can be broken down into subparts, revisited and reworked in a way that is not always possible with physical materials. We are not suggesting you ever substitute opportunities for physical experiences (eg painting) but that you complement them (eg adding effects to an image on a graphics programme) in your classroom. The power of digital technologies is about task transformation not replication (eg typing out), as Belshaw says, it is about '*achieving something new that was previously either impossible or out of reach*' without the tool (2011, p 212). Additionally, digital technologies can sometimes carry out processes more efficiently, freeing up time and cognitive space for other activities. For example, once a child is confident in how to construct a bar chart and the symbolic representation of numeric data, is there any further gain in always doing this, when using a spreadsheet charting function might free up time for analysis?

To recap:

* Payton and Hague (2010) detail creativity as a component of digital literacy: '*the ability to think creatively and imaginatively, and to use technology to create outputs and represent knowledge in different formats and modes*' (p 6);

* Hobbs suggests individuals can '*create content in a variety of forms, making use of language, images, sound, and new digital tools and technologies*' (2010).

The following sections of this chapter explore interpretations of creativity and how these translate when you are working with digital content. A quick online search reveals there are many thousands of productive digital tools available in the form of software for PCs and lap-tops; even more apps (applications) for the iPad or tablet, phablets and smartphones; and a multitude of cloud or online services for producing content. The possibilities can feel daunt-ing so rather than provide a never-ending list of *to try* products you will be encouraged to start by examining the purpose of the task. Once you are clear on the purpose of a task there will be a discussion of the generic/umbrella terms for what tool will help for that particular purpose. No doubt you will want to try out some of these tools so a few suggestions will be made but there are many tools with similar functionality currently available and new tools constantly appear. Often there will be a free version you can obtain or a 30-day trial to enable you to explore whether you think it could make a useful contribution in your classroom.

Schools and classrooms vary greatly in terms of what technology is available day-to-day for learners to utilise. Not only in terms of what, but also how it is deployed. Chapter 2 high-lighted that a true measure of quantity goes beyond listing what is purchased by a school to identifying what level of use there is. We would argue that usage and deployment often have a marked impact beyond the volume of technology purchased. The critical questions below challenge you to explore this statement.

Critical questions

»   *Is technology dispersed throughout the school or centralised in a designated area? Consider what impact this has on children's learning experiences with technology.*

»   *Is the technology freely accessible to learners or are there gatekeepers (teachers/ assistants/technicians) for gaining access? How do the protocols for access enable or hinder independent learning with technology?*

»   *Are children allowed to bring in their own devices? Identify issues this would raise or solve.*

»   *Is access to technology restricted to certain subjects and what is the rationale behind this?*

»   *Is technology used to support inclusion and personalisation? If not, how could it be and what difference could this make to individual learners?*

Rather than list the various combinations of equipment that exist, this chapter assumes that teachers and learners have access to a tool for:

*   capturing static and moving images;

*   recording audio;

*   projecting/accessing content to/on a screen;

*   WiFi internet access;

*   applications or software to

    –   browse the internet

    –   process data

- produce graphs

- edit images, audio and video

- process text with multimedia capacity.

At one end of the spectrum there will be classrooms where every child has their own iPad/tablet, fantastic WiFi and clusters of PCs/Macs. You might want to search for images for the term *classrooms of the future* online or look at the section of Professor Heppell's site *Learning spaces and places* (rubble.heppell.net/places/default.html) to imagine what it could be like.

Even with a few basic pieces of kit there is plenty you can do. Also the more you actually use, experiment and innovate with what you have the more likely your school's budget holders will be persuaded to invest in more.

Creating content and the national curriculum

The importance of creativity is underlined in the opening statement of the computing curriculum:

> *A high-quality computing education equips pupils to understand and change the world through logical thinking and creativity.*

(DfE, 2013, p 188)

The statement continues to articulate the importance of computing to equip '*pupils to use information technology to create programs, systems and a range of media*' (DfE, 2013, p 188). Reference is made to creating programs, systems and a range of media. For example, at Key Stage 1, '*create and debug simple programs*' (DfE, 2013, p 189). The scope of this book on digital literacy is largely situated within the range of media component. The place of programming as a creative activity will be explored as a general principle in this chapter but we will recommend a specialist text at the end of the chapter.

We would also like to highlight the '*develop ideas through information and communication technology*' phrase. You should explore *process* and *product* tools for children to be '*creative users of information and communication technology*' (DfE, 2013, p 188).

The programmes of study for Key Stage 1 and 2 expand, stating that pupils should be taught to (emphasis added by the author):

- KS1 – *use technology purposefully to* **create***, organise, store, manipulate and retrieve digital content*

- KS2 – *select, use and* **combine** *a variety of* **software (including internet services)** *on a* **range of digital devices** *to accomplish given goals, including* **collecting***,* **analysing***, evaluating and* **presenting data** *and* **information***.*

(DfE, 2013, p 189)

As detailed in Chapter 1, information is taken as meaning any symbolic representation of meaning in any form; including numbers, text, visual artefacts and sound. The programmes of study also suggest multimodality in the use of the term *combine*. This may take place using PC/laptop-based software, apps on smartphones, phablets (a tablet sized phone), tablets and online. *Collection* and *analyses* are highlighted because there are many digital tools that can be utilised in the process phase of creating digital content. The analysis above relates to the computing programmes of study but, as reiterated throughout the book, for children's learning tasks to have maximum impact they need to be as authentic and purposeful as possible. Therefore, we would suggest you teach digital literacy components in a cross-curricular and holistic context, acknowledging the need to address development of functional capability at key points in the process.

Creating content and the Teachers' Standards

In relation to technology enhanced learning and teaching, previous chapters have acknowledged the impact technology can have in motivating learners.

You will no doubt have practical classroom opportunities to use technology to '*foster and maintain pupils' interest*' in subjects by the '*provision of an engaging curriculum*' (DfE, 2011, p 10). Further, the Teachers' Standards emphasise acknowledging individual '*dispositions, understanding of how pupils learn*', and '*factors that can inhibit pupils' ability to learn and how best to overcome these*' (DfE, 2011, pp 11–13). Technology is another variable at your disposal as a teacher that can have a dramatic and empowering pedagogical impact.

Defining creativity

Critical question

» *What is creative about each of these activities? Do you consider one more creative than the others and why?*

  – *composing music*

  – *creating a picture*

  – *making a film*

  – *creating a computer program.*

Some of you will not see yourself as creative, you probably view being creative as desirable but you are not entirely sure how you would define it. You may know someone who is musical or artistic and you think they are creative. We think it is worth spending a few minutes exploring what we mean by creativity and putting it into context so that you can practically tackle this dimension of digital literacy.

Reading the following definition of creativity you are reminded to not always focus on the finished product; there are key behaviours and attitudes in the creative process. The Qualifications and Curriculum Authority (QCA) '*emphasised creativity in terms of purpose-*

ful shaping of imagination, producing original and valuable outcomes'. Specifically, QCA *'suggested that creativity involves pupils in thinking or behaviour that involves':*

- *questioning and challenging*
- *making connections, seeing relationships*
- *envisaging what might be*
- *exploring ideas, keeping options open*
- *reflecting critically on ideas, actions, outcomes.*

(2000, cited by Craft in Wilson, 2009, p 9)

Similarly the 2006 Roberts Review expanded on the mindset, values and attitudes that are important:

- *creativity involves thinking or behaving imaginatively;*
- *this imaginative activity is purposeful: that is, it is directed to achieving an objective;*
- *this process must generate something original;*
- *the outcome must be of value in relation to the objective.*

(DCMS/DfES, 2006, p 4, cited by Craft in Wilson, 2009, p 13)

You could interpret the first two points as relating to the creative process and the last two more directly to the product of that process.

We think it worth pausing on the phrase *original*. You may have a very traditional interpretation of *original*, perhaps from academic discussion of plagiarism or news of copyright breeches in the media. Commonly we interpret *original* as being solely the person's own work. Digital technology muddies the water here to some extent, and will do so increasingly we believe. In Chapter 7 rights and responsibilities of being a digital citizen will be explored including, for example, copyright and the advent of new licensing forms such as Creative Commons licences. For now, Belshaw's discussion in Chapter 1 prompts us to remember that in the digital world creating something new might include *'remixing content from other sources'* ... we now need to be aware *'for what purposes content can be appropriated, reused and remixed'* (2011, p 209). Creative Commons licensing is becoming popular and offers the option for digital content copyright to go beyond the familiar *all rights reserved* outright ban, to allow authors to specify how they are happy for their content to be used, ie whether it can be *'copied, distributed, edited, remixed and built upon'* (Creative Commons, 2014).

Multimodal options

Multimodality from a learning perspective was comprehensively explored in theoretical terms in Chapter 3. The use of the term *combine* in the computing curriculum could be taken to imply multimodality (DfE, 2013, p 189). Figure 5.1 begins (it could be extended) to break down what the possible forms of digital content might be.

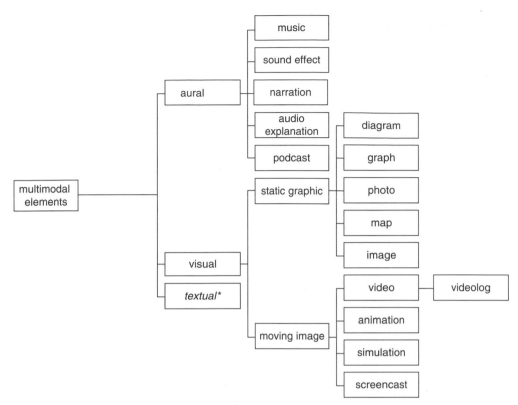

Figure 5.1 *Potential multimodal forms*

In the classroom there is opportunity to create digital artefacts in a range of modes; add in whether components include remixed and repurposed elements, then the options are very considerable. You may be looking for the ultimate list of the perfect educational applications but unfortunately this isn't possible as it depends on many contextual features (age of children, resources available, cost, safeguarding, etc), the nature of the learning task and, of course, the continuous development of new and evolving digital tools. So what is a useful way for you to navigate the options? One option might be to take each element in turn from Figure 5.1 and list what your school has available.

We have not expanded on 'textual' in Figure 5.1 as many tools for creating text allow you to add multimodal elements. For example, Figure 5.2 illustrates some of the diverse tools/ forms that children may use for writing.

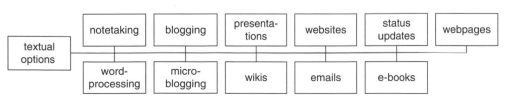

Figure 5.2 *Potential forms for hosting text*

A digital taxonomy

Another approach for deciding which digital tools to utilise can be seen on the popular wiki *Educational Origami* by Churches (2014). Here Bloom's original cognitive taxonomy has been interpreted from a digital technology perspective. Anderson's work in the 1990s moved *creating* to the highest level in terms of thinking skills (Churches, 2014). Churches expands that:

> *Before we can create we must have remembered, understood, applied, analysed and evaluated.*

> (2014)

Therefore, teachers and children can be creating digitally by:

> *designing, constructing, planning, inventing, devising, making, programming, filming, animating, blogging, video blogging, mixing, remixing, wiki-ing, publishing, videocasting, podcasting, directing /producing, building or compiling mashups.*

> (Churches, 2014)

Creative tools

Critical questions

» *Which of these tools for creating content in Table 5.1 have you used before? Perhaps tick using a selected colour.*

» *On what device did you use them? PC, laptop, iPad/tablet, smartphone, phablet or online service? Add initials for the device on to your table.*

» *Using a different colour tick those tools you have enabled children you are working with to use. Similarly, which devices were involved?*

» *Do you regularly use a wider range of tools and devices in your personal life than in your teaching?*

Table 5.1 *Creative tools for education*

social bookmarking services	avatar creation tools	mapping tools	concept-mapping tools	filming and editing
creating animations	making diagrams	taking photos and image manipulation	blogging	wiki-ing
creating e-books	creating a webpage/website	presentation tools	non-photo image creation	graphing/ charting
screen-casting	video-blogging	microblogging	audio recording and editing	audio blogging
podcast creation and broadcast	interactive whiteboard pages	discussion thread		

One explanation might be that educational institutions can lag in the adoption of new technologies: perhaps because of resistance to change and favouring of traditional methods, and no doubt financial investment in hardware is a factor. Even when those barriers are overcome and the school has purchased a class set of iPads or tablets, if these are shared devices there is often red tape to overcome in terms of user accounts when purchasing apps, etc.

With digital tools there are several general trends to be acknowledged. Traditionally software was purchased to install on our PCs and laptops; increasingly online versions of these tools are being used; for example, MS Office suite and Office 365. This may be because of price, as some online versions are free to use. Or it might be the affordance of being able to logon and access files anywhere on a variety or personal and public devices. Previously, storage and backup happened on physical devices; increasingly we have to access cloud (online) storage, backup and syncing between devices. A choice in device is made depending on the nature of the task. You might write an extended piece on a laptop/PC but compose brief emails on your tablet or smartphone. For everyday purposes you probably use your tablet/smartphone camera rather than your digital camera. We buy more services online and increasingly purchase our software as apps. Chapter 9 on e-safety includes a review of research on the devices and services primary-aged children are typically using.

First, we explore two content types that perhaps blur the boundary between process and product, social bookmarking and concept mapping.

Social bookmarking

A social bookmarking service enables you *'to save and share your bookmarks on the web instead of solely on your computer's hard drive'* (Poore, 2013, pp 131–2). It is a way of organising web-based resources beyond your traditional favourites list located on your PC/laptop. In the classroom this could be a useful way to provide lists of websites and resources on a topic with learners. Similarly, children may use social bookmarking to share their search strategies with you and their peers; this gives you valuable insight into the children's ability to locate, organise information and links they are making.

At first you may primarily consider social bookmarking as a process tool but a content output is created; there are options for personalisation and organisation; you have control over keeping content private or publishing it; there may also be options for collaboration. Many, originally web-based, social bookmarking services are now complemented by applications for tablets and smartphones. Typically a *bookmarklet* add-on is also available to add to your web browser to improve ease of use.

As a teacher you may be interested in tools such as Delicious (see delicious.com), described as *'a free and easy tool to save, organise and discover interesting links on the web'*. However, in the user terms it states that users need to be 13 years or older. We would interpret this as a safeguarding disclaimer and an indication that content is not moderated, contact from unknown persons may be possible and you must sign up for a user account. Safeguarding is considered in Chapters 8 and 9 but if you are planning to recommend a service for learners to use you must consider age and e-safety thoroughly. Other popular tools such as Scoop. it and Pinterest also currently require users to be 13 years of age; please check the terms regularly for updated information.

One alternative might be Diigo where it is possible to have school-wide managed accounts for teachers and students. Diigo articulates its purpose as a streamlining tool:

> *Much of our information consumption and research, whether at home or at work, has shifted online ... Yet the workflow with information, from browsing, reading, researching, annotating, storing, organising, remembering, collaborating, sharing, to connecting dots into knowledge, is still largely ad-hoc and inefficient. Diigo is here to streamline the information workflow and dramatically improve your productivity.*

(2014, www.diigo.com/about)

Some really nice pedagogic features include annotation tools when reading, and outdated links are avoided as archived copies of web pages are kept.

An *effective group knowledge repository* can be built when set up as an education user (Diigo, 2014).

There has been a fairly comprehensive consideration of an educational context and some safeguarding assurances are given at www.diigo.com/teacher_entry/educationupgrades. Unlike some other services, approved teachers can set up student accounts with the necessary safeguarding issues addressed.

CASE STUDY

Diigo statement regarding student accounts (2014)

Student accounts are Diigo accounts created by approved teachers through their Teacher Console. Note that accounts created through the normal sign-up process are NOT student accounts. Student accounts have the following special settings to protect the privacy and safety of students.

- *Classmates in the same class are automatically added as friends with one another to facilitate communication, but students cannot add anyone else as friends except through email.*

- *Students can only communicate with their friends and teachers. No one except their friends can send message, group invite, or write on their profile wall.*

- *Student profiles will not be indexed for People Search, nor made available to public search engines.*

(help.diigo.com/teacher-account/faq)

Evernote might be one to watch in the future but it is not currently directed at children. Some protocols are detailed for a school, suggesting obtaining parental consent (you can read more at evernote.com/legal/tos.php under 'Can kids use Evernote?').

Concept mapping

Many of you will be familiar with using concept mapping with children as a tool for representing connections and understanding in a range of subjects. Many learners prefer to create visual representations of their understanding and knowledge; digital versions offer opportunities for revision and reworking, possibilities for including hypertext, and sharing with a wider audience. Functionality is similar across tools and this section includes two suggestions if you are not familiar with digital concept mapping.

Popplet is a popular concept-mapping tool with teachers (see popplet.com). However, again the minimum user age is stated as13. Even when using tools suggested on popular educators' blogs you need to be aware of the terms and potential safeguarding issues (eg www.educatorstechnology.com/2012/06/18-free-mind-mapping-tools-for-teachers.html).

A concept-mapping suite of programs you might want to explore is the *Inspiration* software series that is dedicated to visual learning (www.inspiration.com/visual-learning/mind-mapping). As with many of the suggested programs a free 30-day trial is available as a download. With *Inspiration* three options are available (www.inspiration.com/freetrial); including *Webspiration Classroom* for teachers; *Inspiration 9* for ages eight and up; and *Kidspiration* for ages 4–9. *Inspiration maps* and *Kidspiration* are also available as applications for tablets and smartphones.

The popular primary software producer 2Simple also have *2Connect* (see www.2simple.com/component/virtuemart/age-group/5–7/2connect-downloadable-detail?Itemid=0).

Static images

In your classroom you may be asking children to express themselves through static images in various subjects: either in creating images as the final product or to support a curriculum topic. This might involve using a digital camera and then editing and manipulating images. Using painting applications to replicate real life processes and skills or creating maps, plans, images using an object based drawing package. Each form will be detailed below and some suggested software and applications briefly explored. Chapter 4 on *Information literacy* provided brief explanations of static image file formats and the implications for use.

Photo editing

In today's media-rich world it is incredibly important for children to be able to critically appraise the images they come into contact with. For visual literacy it is important to understand how a digital image can be captured and heavily edited before publication. When working with upper Key Stage 2 children resources such as the Dove Evolution video (www.youtube.com/watch?v=hibyAJOSW8U) series can be very powerful for children to watch and see the degree to which magazine pictures are digitally enhanced. Allowing children the opportunity to simulate this process by manipulating and enhancing photos themselves is the most powerful way of getting children to fully appreciate how common and easy it is. Most graphic packages will allow you to import photos, annotate (eg labels to create a diagram), apply effects, and superimpose images by creating layers. iPhoto or Google Picasa are popular photo editing and collating services; there are many others so you can select a tool where there are age-appropriate tools.

Critical question

» *Can you identify what personal, social and health education opportunities exist when exploring how images can be altered?*

Painting

Many of you will be familiar with programs that seek to replicate real life painting. A range of tools including brushes, spray tools, fill, shapes, stamps, etc are available and you can paint in watercolour, oil paint, etc. You can often cut/copy and paste to create tiled patterns and draw over imported images. A nice early map-making activity is drawing over a simple aerial photograph. Free examples suitable for adults and older primary-aged children include *MS Paint* and *Paint.net* (www.getpaint.net/index.html) for PCs/laptops. In terms of apps *Drawing with Carl* is very intuitive for younger children. *Art of Glow, DooDoo Pad* and *Kaleidoscope Drawing Pad* apps are great for creating bright patterns. *Fingerpaint Magic* works well with younger children and it emphasises the direct finger–to-effect relationship for younger children using an iPad or tablet. *ArtSet* offers something more sophisticated and a few others worth exploring for different age groups include: *Hello Oil painter, SketchBook Express, DoodleBuddy* and *DrawFree*.

Object-based drawing

Some of the painting applications suggested above will also be suitable for simple technical drawing. However, in Key Stage 2 there may be occasions when you would like to utilise an object-based drawing package to create detailed maps, plans, diagrams and more technical drawings. *Open Office Draw* and *Google Docs Drawing* programs are more suited to these types of projects in primary. *Google SketchUp* is available for 3D modelling but probably only suitable in an upper Key Stage 2 primary classroom.

Moving images

In relation to creating videos you need to capture, edit and share the content. The moving images might take the form of video, stop frame animation, animation or a screencast. In terms of publication your school may have hosting capacity on their VLE or webpage. One alternative is TeacherTube: accounts can only be held by those aged over 18, but there is some functionality for creating *classrooms* (www.teachertube.com). An overview of moving image file formats was given in Chapter 4.

Stop frame animation

> Stop motion (also known as stop frame) is an animation technique to make a physically manipulated object appear to move on its own. The object is moved in small increments between individually photographed frames, creating the illusion of movement when the series of frames is played as a continuous sequence.

> (en.wikipedia.org/wiki/Stop_motion)

Stop frame animation is a form of video popular in primary schools for a range of projects: for example, recreating the lifecycle of a tadpole, retelling a famous story or creative storytelling. The video footage can often be augmented with text titles, sound effects, music, narration and special effects. Often a specialist programme is best for this form of video creation.

I Can Animate is a popular program and now there are applications for the iPad and iPhone. A free trial is available as a download (see www.kudlian.net/products/icananimate/). A recent collaboration with Aardman Animation Ltd (of Wallace and Gromit fame) is *Animate it* (see www.animate-it.com). You can usually find examples on TeacherTube in advance to show children. Another suggestion is the iMotion app; *'iMotion is an intuitive and powerful time-lapse and stop-motion app for iOS'* (www.fingerlab.net/website/Fingerlab/iMotion_HD.html). The *Kar2ouche Primary Creative Toolkit* is also popular and is described as *'creative role-play, picture making, storyboarding and animation software'* (www.immersiveeducation.eu/index.php/kar2ouchepg).

Other approaches to animation

Other approaches to animation do not always involve recording video although you can often import still images and export the finished product as a video file.

*   At the simplest level it could be animating an object in Textease Studio CT to move around the screen (www.rm.com/shops/whatwedo/Product.aspx?cref=PD3756602).

*   Another piece of software to explore is *2Animate* from 2Simple (www.2simple.com/component/virtuemart/age-group/3–5/2animate-downloadable-detail?Itemid=0).

*   Apps to explore include: *Toontastic Junior* (www.launchpadtoys.com/toontasticjr/) and *PuppetPalsHD* (www.polishedplay.com).

*   You may also be interested in avatar creators (eg *Morfo* (www.morfoapp.com)), they can be great fun for primary children. Typically you can import a photo or create a character onscreen which you then get to move and add speech.

Video editing

For video editing most schools will have access to iMovie and/or Moviemaker (Windows) as part of the Windows Live Essentials (see windows.microsoft.com/en-gb/windows-live/essentials). There are extensive tutorial materials online for both products.

Screencasting

Screencasting is when you record what is happening on your computer screen, usually with narration; this is particularly useful for detailed explanations and allowing children to access these instructions at home or school. Children can then pause, replay or skip through according at their own pace. A few popular screen-recording tools include:

*   Camtasia (www.techsmith.com/camtasia.html);

*   CamStudio (camstudio.org);

*   Screenr (www.screenr.com);

*   Screen-o-matic (www.screencast-o-matic.com).

There are now versions for iPads and tablets including:

*   ShowMe (www.showme.com);

*   ScreenChomp (www.techsmith.com/screenchomp.html);

*   Educreations (www.educreations.com).

Audio

In relation to recording, editing and sharing audio there are several options. On the simplest level many word-processors and presentation packages allow you to directly record narration using an inexpensive USB microphone or import sound clips. There are many video tutorials on YouTube or the links below are useful for MS products:

*   adding sound to *PowerPoint* (office.microsoft.com/en-gb/powerpoint-help/add-and-play-sounds-in-a-presentation-HA001230305.aspx);

*   adding sound to *Word* (office.microsoft.com/en-gb/word-help/insert-a-sound-HP005257344.aspx).

A simple, portable, MP3 recording device, for example an Easi-speak (see www.tts-group.co.uk/shops/tts/Products/PD1727034/Easi-Speak-MP3-Recorder-Player/) can be a powerful alternative recording tool for a child with transcription difficulties; for example, in a science lesson where the learning objective is not writing focused. There are numerous simple recording devices where export and editing are not required, eg recordable postcards, pegs, talking tins, photo albums, talking clipboards, etc. These give children a very accessible tool for recording ideas overcoming any barriers transcription might present. The TTS website given above is a treasure trove of ideas for the classroom.

On a more sophisticated level you may be creating audio with multiple tracks or layers that you want to be able to manipulate and then export or publish. Chapter 4 explains the main types of audio file formats you are likely to encounter. When using existing audio and sound effects ensure the copyright provisions allow you to sample and remix. Searching via Creative Commons at search.creativecommons.org will list a number of music databases.

- For music creation, programs such as Garageband are very popular. '*GarageBand turns your iPad, iPhone and iPod touch into a collection of Touch Instruments and a fully featured recording studio – so you can make music anywhere you go*' (itunes. apple.com/gb/app/garageband/id408709785?mt=8).

- Beatwave is a music creation app that '*lets you make amazing music simply by tapping. Create songs anywhere, anytime on your iPhone or iPad*' (beatwave.co).

- A popular free recorder and editor is Audacity (audacity.sourceforge.net). An overview of the features is given at audacity.sourceforge.net/about/features.

- A popular app is WavePad Audio Editor: '*A free sound editor for recording, editing, adding effects, and sending audio, WavePad allows you to record voice or music, then edit the recording and add effects to achieve high quality audio recordings*' (www.nchsoftware.com/software/index.html).

Writing

Figure 5.2 illustrated some of the forms writing may take using some of the Web 2.0 tools available and newer offerings in the form of e-book creators that are lovely to use on an iPad/tablet with children. One of the most powerful dimensions to digital writing is the ease of publishing it to an audience, often giving children a sense they are writing for a real purpose. Chapter 6 will explore in detail tools (eg wikis) that can make collaboration within and beyond the classroom very accessible. Blogging is mentioned here briefly but will also be explored in Chapter 6 alongside wikis and podcasting. We believe that wikis, blogs and podcasts are three very accessible forms for the primary classroom worthy of more detailed consideration.

Creating websites, e-books and comics are other text-based forms considered here. As reiterated throughout the book, do check the terms of reference carefully to ensure they are suitable for primary-aged children and what safeguarding measures are in place. Where possible use an educational version with school-created accounts. Many VLEs also now offer tools for creating blogs, wikis and e-portfolios where the teacher can control collaboration and sharing possibilities within the administrative settings.

Blogging

Blogging will be explored in detail in Chapter 6 as it a very accessible and powerful writing tool for primary-aged children. A number of examples from schools are included for you to explore. For now, a blog can be defined as:

> Resembling a diary or a journal, a blog is normally a chronologically organised series of entries composed of text, images, video and even interactive content ... in addition to this the blog is also characterised by hypertext,links, in other words that connect them to other blogs or other pages on the web.

> (Poore, 2013, p 3)

Your school may already have a blogging tool as part of their VLE, which may be suitable and the most appropriate tool to use in the classroom. Depending on the circumstances the VLE may offer reassurance in terms of public access. On the other hand, the example of Martha's blog in Chapter 6 highlights the impact an audience can have. If you have equipped learners with the appropriate e-safety protocols for using open access blogging tools, there are four Poore (2013) recommends:

- Blogger.com (accessed via a Google account);

- Tumblr.com (www.tumblr.com);

- Wordpress.com (wordpress.com);

- KidBlog.org (kidblog.org/home/).

KidBlog is certainly worth exploring as you will have greater control over who can access and interact with children via their blogs. You always need to check the small print carefully but dedicated educational provision should be your first choice where possible with primary-aged children.

> *Kidblog is designed for K-12 teachers who want to provide each student with an individual blog. Students publish posts and participate in academic discussions within a secure classroom blogging community. Teachers maintain complete control over student blogs and user accounts.*
>
> (kidblog.org/home/)

Poore (2013) also provides some guidance on how to scaffold student blogging and genre features (pp 55–6). Poore continues to suggest approaches to marking written content for this form and what might included in a rubric for assessment purposes (2013, pp 56–8).

Wikis

Wikis are also a key focus of Chapter 6 where their role as a collaborative learning tool is considered, their educational value assessed and a typology of wikis presented. In addition, a range of existing school and primary appropriate wikis are listed for you to explore. If you are not already familiar with a wiki and the process of construction a simple explanation follows.

> *The contributor to a wiki uses a simple WYSIWYG editor, which they access by clicking a button on the page itself, to generate new pages or edit existing ones within the wiki site. In addition to this hyperlinks are used very heavily to connect pages into an interlinking resource ... in this manner they draw on the power of the web to connect people, but the emphasis in wikis falls on active and direct collaboration between members of the online community.*
>
> (Poore, 2013, p 4)

Barber and Cooper (2012) detail a nice example of introducing a Year 6 class to using a wiki to create a class resource about the solar system (pp 92–3). Encouraging children to create wikis themselves is the most powerful way to understand how they work and the advantages and disadvantages. Many children will have encountered Wikipedia, and rather than declaring it *good* (ie democratic and collaborative knowledge building) or *bad* (ie anyone can edit it), understanding how the tool functions is key.

Wikispaces, in particular the, Wikispaces Classroom option again offers some education focused features that are worth exploring (www.wikispaces.com/content/classroom). Poore (2013) also suggests PBWorks.com and offers detailed guidance on choosing a wiki service (pp 68–9). For further suggestions see Chapter 6.

E-books

> *An electronic book is a book-length publication in digital form, consisting of text, images, or both, readable on computers or other electronic devices. Although sometimes defined as 'an electronic version of a printed book', many e-books exist without any printed equivalent.*
>
> (en.wikipedia.org/wiki/E-book)

In relation to e-books there are many published examples, in a range of file formats, some can be accessed on any device and others require a particular e-reader. In terms of functionality an e-book will have some or all of the following features.

- The option to '*translate into different languages*', this may be useful in the classroom where some learners will have English as a second language.

- The ability to '*display motion, enlarge or change fonts*' can be supportive in providing inclusive access for learners.

- In addition, devices with '*text-to-speech*' capabilities mean that the text can be read aloud to children. This could be invaluable to a learner who has knowledge and understanding on a topic but is limited by their reading ability; for example, due to having dyslexia.

- In relation to efficient information processing, the ability to '*search for key terms*' can be a useful addition in lengthier documents.

- A similar scaffolding tool for learners is where they can instantly access definitions for unfamiliar terminology.

- Some e-books will include the option for '*highlighting and annotation*' on the text replicating the process many of us use when looking at paper-based sources.

- Readers are not limited to a '*linear pathway*' and the inclusion of '*hypertext can allow for personalised pathways*' through the material.

- '*Non-textual multimedia can be embedded including widgets, images, videos, audio files and multimedia content*'.

- Navigation can include '*flipping or scrolling*' gestures (en.wikipedia.org/wiki/E-book).

It is worth remembering that being able to create text and include images or other multi-modal components is not new; you have been able to do this with desktop publishing software for many years. Even if you don't have access to the e-book creators listed below there are examples of children producing simple e-books with software such as *MS Publisher*, *PowerPoint* and *Word* or equivalent (see olc.spsd.sk.ca/DE/PD/ebooks/background.html).

However, an e-book application creates a satisfying and polished final product that can be shared widely. Text and image pages are created and audio narration can usually be added. Four recommended e-book creators to explore are:

- Book Creator (www.redjumper.net/bookcreator/); there are some examples to explore at www.redjumper.net/blog/category/education/;

- Creative Book Builder (getcreativebookbuilder.blogspot.co.uk);

- Myebook (www.myebook.com/index.php);

- Story Creator (itunes.apple.com/gb/app/story-creator-easy-story-book/id545369477?mt=8).

Websites

In the past creating websites was out of the reach of many primary-aged children. Simple tools such as Weebly are popular with teachers but require users to be 13 years of age. Again it is recommended that you use the education version (at education.weebly.com). Just-2-easy (J2e) was created with primary-aged children in mind and allows asynchronous collaboration (www.j2e.com/lgfl).

Comics

Two comic book creators worth exploring include *Comic Life*, also available as an app (plasq.com/products/comiclife/ios) and *Toontastic* (www.launchpadtoys.com/toontastic/), which creates cartoon style art and wording over photos and videos.

Programming

The national curriculum makes reference to children creating programs and systems. Computational thinking is often considered a creative problem-solving process. Resnick argues that all children can benefit from learning to code; first, that it helps them understand their media-rich world and second that it offers an outlet for creative expression (2013). Coding is viewed as an extension of writing as 'the ability to code allows you to write new types of things – interactive stories, games, animations and simulations' (Resnick, 2013). Resnick underlines the importance that children learn effectively when they are working on 'personally meaningful projects' where personalisation is key and in Scratch afforded by creating, importing and 'mixing graphics, animations, photos, music and sound' (2012a).

- Scratch – a tool for creating games and animations uses a child-friendly visual programming language supported within an online community and a wealth or resources and examples. Scratch can be used online or downloaded (scratch.mit.edu).

- 2Code is offered as part of PurpleMash by 2 Simple (www.2simple.com/news#8260).

- CoderDojo describes itself as 'the open source, volunteer led, global movement of free coding clubs for young people' (coderdojo.com).

- Similarly, Code Academy is most suited to upper Key Stage 2 children with some basic coding capability (www.codecademy.com).

- Code Club is 'a nationwide network of volunteer-led after school coding clubs for children aged 9–11' (www.codeclub.org.uk).

For younger children exploring creating simple programs:

- Beebot – there is now an app to complement this popular classroom resource (www.tts-group.co.uk/shops/tts/content/view.aspx?cref=PSGEN2293277&utm_source=BeeBotApp&utm_medium=Advertising&utm_campaign=BeeBotApp);

- Daisy the Dinosaur – a tool for learning the basics of programming (www.mindleaptech.com/apps/daisy-the-dinosaur/);

- Hopscotch (www.gethopscotch.com);

- Cargo-Bot (twolivesleft.com/CargoBot/).

Critical points

» *New applications arrive on the market daily and you may find it useful to add a few review sites to your favourites list, especially those which narrow software lists down to subjects, primary-age age phases, etc. One to get you started is www. apps4primaryschools.co.uk. Some of these may be commercial sites but they serve as a starting point.*

» *Similarly, technology-in-education blogs are another area for you to hear about new tools and classroom applications. However, you still need to check the terms of reference carefully in relation to privacy options, audience, ownership, permitted age of use and whether tailored-for-education versions exist.*

» *Using digital tools can be exciting and motivating for children and teachers but we would advise you always step back and consider the pedagogical benefits and issues involved. Sometimes technology isn't the best way to accomplish a goal.*

Further reading and useful resources

The Educational Origami wiki by Churches gives a comprehensive overview of learning and teaching with digital technologies and suggests tools to use: edorigami.wikispaces.com/Traditional+and+Digital+Practice. The wiki is not written with primary-aged children in mind so you will need to reflect on the transferable components.

To read more on computing and children creating simple programs we would recommend:

Bird, J, Caldwell, H and Mayne, P (eds) (2014) *Lessons in Teaching Computing*. Learning Matters.

In terms of social media and web tools we would recommend:

Poore, M (2013) *Using Social Media in the Classroom*. Sage.

Barber, D and Cooper, L (2012) *Using New Web Tools in the Primary Classroom*. Routledge.

References

Barber, D and Cooper, L (2012) *Using New Web Tools in the Primary Classroom*. Routledge.

Belshaw, D (2011) *What is 'Digital Literacy'?* [online] Available at: neverendingthesis.com/doug-belshaw-edd-thesis-final.pdf (accessed 31 October 2014).

Churches, A (no date) Educational Origami Wiki: Bloom's Digital Taxonomy. [online] Available at: edorigami.wikispaces.com/Bloom's+Digital+Taxonomy (accessed 31 October 2014).

Creative Commons (2014) About the Licenses. [online] Available at: creativecommons.org/licenses/ (accessed 31 October 2014).

Department for Education (2011) *Teachers' Standards: Guidance for School Leaders, School Staff and Governing Bodies*. [online] Available at: www.gov.uk/government/uploads/system/uploads/attachment_data/file/301107/Teachers__Standards.pdf (accessed 31 October 2014).

Department for Education (2013) *The National Curriculum in England: Dramework Document*. [online] Available at: www.gov.uk/government/uploads/system/uploads/attachment_data/file/210969/NC_framework_document_-_FINAL.pdf (accessed 31 October 2014).

Hobbs, R (2010) *Digital and Media Literacy: A Plan of Action*. [online] Available at: www.knight-comm.org/wp-content/uploads/2010/12/Digital_and_Media_Literacy_A_Plan_of_Action.pdf (accessed 31 October 2014).

Payton, S and Hague, C (2010) *Digital Literacy in Practice: Case Studies of Primary and Secondary Classrooms*. Futurelab. [online] Available at: www2.futurelab.org.uk/resources/documents/project_reports/digital_literacy_case_studies.pdf (accessed 31 October 2014).

Poore, M (2013) *Using Social Media in the Classroom*. Sage.

Resnick, M (2012a) Reviving Papert's Dream. *Educational Technology*, 52(4): 42–6. [online] Available at: web.media.mit.edu/~mres/papers/educational-technology-2012.pdf (accessed 31 October 2014).

Resnick, M (2012b) Lifelong Kindergarten. *Cultures of Creativity*, pp 50–2. [online] Available at: web.media.mit.edu/~mres/papers/CulturesCreativityEssay.pdf (accessed 31 October 2014).

Resnick, M (2013) Teaching Kids to Code. [online] Available at: www.edsurge.com/n/2013-05-08-learn-to-code-code-to-learn (accessed 31 October 2014).

Wilson, A (ed) (2009) *Creativity in Primary Education*, 2nd edition. Exeter: Learning Matters Ltd.

6 Collaboration, communication and networking

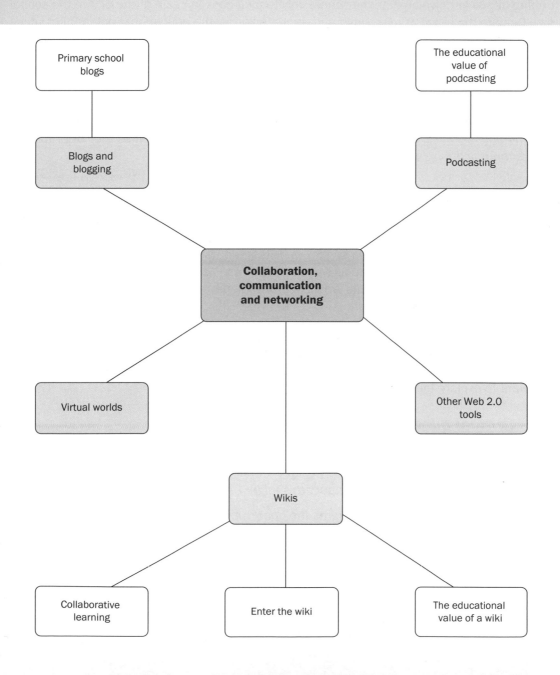

Primary school blogs

Blogs and blogging

The educational value of podcasting

Podcasting

Collaboration, communication and networking

Virtual worlds

Other Web 2.0 tools

Wikis

Collaborative learning

Enter the wiki

The educational value of a wiki

Introduction

The theme of collaboration, communication and networking is central to considerations of effective pedagogy. However, as is typically the case with new inventions and innovative ideas, developments in digital technologies raise questions about the value and use of new media within the school curriculum. For example, you are likely to be concerned with issues of e-safety (Byron, 2008), and the emergence of a cut-and-paste culture (McKenzie, 2008) has also received extended attention. On the other side of the fence several authors have commented on how children are currently required to leave the real world behind as they *unplug* or *power down* on entering school only to plug back in again at the end of the school day. Despite the range of misgivings and apprehensions, the educational potential of social media and new technology is just so great that the inevitable tide of transformation is upon us once more. The value of new media and new technology is also recognised in the national curriculum for computing at Key Stage 2 where direct reference is made to pupils being taught to collaborate and share online. Pupils need to be taught to:

> *understand computer networks including the internet; how they can provide multiple services, such as the world-wide web; and the opportunities they offer for communication and collaboration.*

> (NC, 2013, p 189)

It's now common knowledge that Web 2.0, the internet characterised by participation, where users of the internet are producers as well as consumers, provides multiple opportunities for collaborative learning such as blogging, wikis and podcasting. Primary school children are also able to publish their work via school websites and, when suitably managed, may have their photos and videos uploaded to websites such as Flickr and YouTube or TeacherTube. There are numerous social media applications that have as yet under-realised potential within primary education.

This chapter introduces and discusses various forms of new media for collaboration, communication and networking with a particular focus on blogs, wikis, podcasts and virtual worlds. It also highlights a sample from the range of social media which will act as a starting point if you want to explore this burgeoning area more fully.

Critical questions

» *Review your understanding and experience of social media. Which social media do you use regularly? What are the positive and negatives features? If you don't use social media consider what impact this might have on your teaching.*

» *The national curriculum highlights the opportunities for communicating and collaborating afforded by computer networks such as the internet. Starting with your own experience, make a list of opportunities for communication and collaboration within a primary school context. Consider the advantages, disadvantages and associated risks. NB Chapter 9 focuses on the broader context of e-safety.*

Blogs and blogging

As one of the forms taken by Web 2.0 blogging and the blogosphere are now pervasive features of the world we live in. There are simply millions of blogs and millions upon millions of posts are being uploaded as a continuous stream to these blogs. But what exactly is a blog? In the early days of the internet, the creation of 'web logs', lists of websites worth visiting, were a typical preoccupation of the computer-literate middle-class male (nerd!?). Today, in 2014, no knowledge at all of HTML or computer programming is needed to create or contribute to a blog, the gender mix has become more balanced (Tremayne, 2007) and there are numerous types of blogs rather than just the *web log*. There are microblogs such as Twitter, hyper-local blogs (which focus on the immediate locality of the blogger) and live blogs which report on events as they happen (Chapman, 2013), as well as blogs relating to particular topics or themes, eg fashion blogs, news blogs, video blogs and education related blogs referred to as edublogs.

Richardson (2009) separated the ostensive blogging activity that occurs on websites such as Facebook.com and MySpace.com as journaling rather than blogging, as a new genre of *connective writing* (p 28). Tremayne (2007) shared a similar view when maintaining that blogging will never replace journalism. This suggests a theory of blogging as *gate watching*, a form of citizen journalism that brings the authority of mass media reporting into question.

CASE STUDY

Martha's blog

Perhaps more by chance than design this nonetheless illuminating case study of nine-year-old Martha Payne's *NeverSeconds* blog draws attention to the potential power and consequences of a seemingly innocuous blog (Payne and Payne, 2012). Martha's blog started when she decided to take daily photos of her school dinners and publish them together with a simple rating scale, including *Food-o-meter*, *Health rating* and *Pieces of hair*. Whereas the school was very supportive and there was even expression of support from the world-famous chef Jamie Oliver, the local authority was immediately unfavourably disposed to the blog and the publicity it was receiving. Very soon thousands of emails were being received by the *NeverSeconds* blog and Martha's father set about the task of reading, moderating and responding to the emails. Interest from local newspapers and radio was quickly followed by interest from the national as well as international media. There were continuous and persistent requests to interview Martha as well as offers of lucrative financial deals relating to the blog. Yet the local council continued to express criticism of the blog and the detail of the story identifies various unpleasant accusations including unwarranted claims by the council and employees of the council; Martha was also subjected to bullying at the school.

The blog received more than a million page visits and very soon 'Emails were coming in at more than a 1000 an hour and even the computer was struggling' (p 117). Rather than undermine the serious healthy food message of the blog by agreeing to accept advertising revenue from the blog Martha decided to link the blog to Mary's Meals charity in Malawi. The blog raised more than £120,000 to provide school meals for children in Malawi. Eventually, rather than accept any of the numerous media offers, Martha and members of her family went to Malawi to get first-hand experience which was then reported in the blog. The blog itself was also developed internationally by rotating the management of the blog across children from different countries.

Comment

Pedagogically this is a really interesting example of a cross-curricular authentic learning experience. It also draws attention to some of the issues associated with blogging. For example, Martha signed herself using the pseudonym *Veg* rather than her own name although the newspapers and other mass media managed to discover the author of the blog. Anonymity includes both positive and negative affordances, eg retaliation is possible when the blogger is identifiable whereas anonymity supports challenge to authority. On the other hand anonymity can tempt some bloggers to engage in trolling or flaming by posting threatening, abusive or upsetting remarks. Shaffer (2012) referred to O'Reilly's proposed Code of Conduct for blogging which banned unacceptable content, gave support to private responding to controversial comments and use of a website code of conduct badge, eg *civility enforced* or *anything goes*. However, Shaffer (2012) emphasised the unmanageability of a code of conduct contrasted with a self-regulation approach and noted that '*With no designated editors and obvious biases, interactive blog sites can be sarcastic, cynical and cheeky – all of which make well-written entries entertaining and enlightening to read*' (p 78). Yet a potential legal issue arises where the moderator of a blog's code of conduct overlooks removal of a libellous post.

Critical question

» *Use the case study of Martha's* NeverSeconds *blog as a starting point for reflecting on issues and implications for setting up a blog within your own primary school context. For example, what can you do to prepare for unexpected consequences?*

Primary school blogs

It's worth noting that public exposure is not a necessary characteristic of blogging in an educational context. Blogging software such as Wordpress.org, Google's Blogger.com or the specifically educational www.j2e.com content management system for schools provide options to restrict access which is able to affect the visibility of the blog, eg private access to registered users only or direct or moderated public accessibility. Using this restricted approach, you could arrange for groups of children to use a shared blog space without potential disturbance from unwelcome outsiders. Blogging within a protected environment can afford children the opportunity to become experts on a particular topic through researching the topic while they continue to contribute to a private access registered users only blog – a sort of Mantle of the Expert approach, with potential recognition and involvement from parents and authorised others.

Table 6.1 Examples of primary school blogs

You can easily locate blogs on the internet by using a search engine.	• www.blogsearchengine.org/ • www.teachthought.com/teaching/52-education-blogs-you-should-follow/
Examples of primary school blogs are useful starting points for creating your own school blog site.	
Chatsworth Primary School includes rules for blogging and blogs for each of the classes as well as for the teachers. The format is that class teachers comment on an event or activity that happened in class, pose a challenge for the week or set homework planning activities and pupils then post their responses.	www.chatsworthprimaryschool.co.uk/blogging/
The approach of Llansannor Church Primary School includes individual children having their own blogs as well as class and teacher blogs and for blogs to be organised in year groups. Children and teachers respond by posting comments. As with Chatsworth, photos and images are used effectively and both are schools where blogging occurs on a regular basis.	www.llansannorschool.net/page/?pid=4
Sudley Junior School divides blogs into 'Grown up blogs' and 'Children's blogs'. Open access is restricted to the latest blogs in the grown-up section where it is also possible to read children's comments. All other areas of the blog are password protected.	sudley-junior-school.primaryblog.net/
The Deans Primary School Blogsite was created using the popular www.wordpress.com and features numerous images and image transitions, embedded video clips and separate areas for a clubs blog, well done blog and class blogs.	thedeansprimary.wordpress.com/

Critical questions

» School blogs come in all shapes and sizes: consider the advantages and drawbacks of a blog with a high visual impact contrasted with a more text-based blog.

» Browse through a range of primary school blogs and detail the practical issues of maintaining an up-to-date blog.

Wikis

The exponential rate of growth in the world's knowledge that characterises the digital age means that your teaching should focus on *flexible, generative knowledge*. Miyake (2007) focuses on collaborative learning as a means to this end, noting that this involves '*making things visible, shareable, reflectable, and modifiable by the participating learners*' (p 249).

Reflecting more broadly, social networking has been identified as a characteristic of the '*net generation*' (Tapscott, 2009) which suggests today's teenagers are already predisposed to a more collaborative approach to learning. West and West (2009) describe '*millennials*', those born after 1982, as social, digitally literate, networked team players who value instant feedback and authentic learning experiences. And new literacies which involve producing remixes and mashups also draw upon the collective wisdom made accessible via digital technology and the internet.

Collaborative learning

Watkins (2009) drew a simple distinction between co-operative and collaborative learning. Where pupils work co-operatively they work on their own individual tasks, pursuing their own goals while supporting others in their group. So, pupils in your Key Stage 1/Key Stage 2 class may respond with three stars and a wish when working with a learning buddy or simply pass the ruler when asked. Collaboration, however, involves working on a shared task with a shared purpose. Miyake (2007) identified several collaborative approaches including knowledge building, articulating thoughts, reciprocal teaching and various forms of the jigsaw method, eg use of expert groups and note-sharing software. Essentially, in the jigsaw method, you start your pupils off as part of an expert group taking responsibility for learning about a particular aspect of a topic and then they join mixed groups to report what they have learnt (www.jigsaw.org). Using the jigsaw method would help you ensure that all pupils have an active role during collaborative group work.

Although a collaborative approach can be incorporated into all curriculum subjects, as a useful starting point Spring (1997) used the phrase *collaborative authoring* to describe a range of different types of collaborative writing, eg where one member of the group produces a plan and draft that is then edited by the whole group or where the whole group produces the plan and draft that is then revised by one group member. The range of approaches to collaborative writing is extensive. For example, sequential writing occurs where group members take turns writing one section after another. This form of collaboration can resemble *chain stories* which are a form of *linear collaborative narrative* (Rettberg, 2012) that can become incoherent when the parts are not sufficiently well related but can also be humorous and imaginative.

Enter the wiki

A *wiki* is essentially a collaborative online space comprising an *Edit* page where content is able to be added and modified by anyone who visits the page; a *page history* which shows changes to the edit page including dates of changes; and a *discussion area* which is useful for tracking the construction of knowledge presented on the edit page. It's interesting that danah boyd (2014) contrasted the authority of Google search results with the content of Wikipedia. In particular she referred to the comment of one teenager who said, '*if I'm looking for something that I want, and it's true, I usually go on Google*' (p 183). Essentially the school had referred to Wikipedia as unreliable and inaccurate and this pupil had '*interpreted this to mean that anything that appeared at the top of the Google search page must be true. If not why would it appear at the top?*' (p 183). As a teacher you are more likely to have a constructivist perspective on learning and knowledge. Wikipedia is a good example of this process in action. Far more significant than results of an internet search for knowledge creation is the development of critical evaluation skills.

Although at first glance the expectation might be that lots of junk, flaming (internet slang for provocative or insulting remarks) and other unacceptable content would find its way onto the wiki, in practice this is not what happens. What generally happens is that the content of the wiki is monitored by designated editors and if a page is completely messed up through blatant vandalism wikis typically have a restore feature which will revert to the previously edited page. There is also usually an option to restrict access to only those who have been allocated a login and password.

The educational value of a wiki

You need to give particular attention to learning outcomes when planning to use a wiki in an educational context. Wikipedia, for example, as an encyclopaedia, provides the reader with a ready-made research report produced by multiple authors. This in itself may support the aim to evaluate content but may undermine a learning objective to search for and locate relevant sources. Learning outcomes may also be subject specific. For instance, from the point of view of tracking the discussion of edited contributions in a history wiki: *'The value of watching this type of activity for students in school is that they can see a form of public history in the making, happening online'* (Messer, 2012, p 48).

Carrington (2009) emphasised the role and value of wikis as part of the participatory culture that characterises the digital world. However, Carrington also emphasised that currently wikis are actually more likely to support established approaches to learning and teaching rather than having a transformative impact. West and West (2009) reinforce the educational value of wikis when adumbrating skills and behaviours associated with being able to use a wiki effectively. In particular they refer to group skills such as being able to communicate effectively, being able to manage conflict and make decisions. They also focus on the need for openness and integrity which relates to developing trust and self-organisation. Richardson (2009, p 61) re-emphasises the value of wikis for learning:

> In using wikis, students are not only learning how to publish content; they are also learning how to develop and use all sorts of collaborative skills, negotiating with others to agree on correctness, meaning, relevance and more. In essence, students begin to teach each other.

Types of wiki

Bloom's taxonomy (West and West, 2009) is one foundation for categorising wikis; another is analysing how wikis are being used in schools (Carrington, 2009). Table 6.2 (overleaf) is a simplified composite of these approaches.

Starting with a blank page is always more difficult than having a scaffolded framework so specifying a task outline, section headings and starting points may be helpful. However, Richardson (2009) has emphasised that *'the more autonomy teachers give to students in*

Table 6.2 Based on the views of West and West (2009) and Carrington (2009)

Using Bloom's taxonomy		Using observed practice	
Examples		Examples	
Knowledge construction	Encyclopaedias Fact files Class dictionaries	Knowledge management	School or class website/webpage created as a wiki
Critical thinking	Book reviews Class discussions Evaluating websites	Narrative builder	Use of wiki for collaborative writing
Contextual application	Collaborative story writing Group problem solving Planning an event	Resource aggregator	This includes use of wiki by teachers to assemble useful links to teaching resources
		Value adding	Additional contributions adding value to existing texts

terms of negotiating the scope and quality of the content they are creating, the better' (p 61). The links in Table 6.3 include examples of approaches and formats based on Table 6.2.

Table 6.3 Links to examples of different types of wiki

Specific examples of wiki encyclopaedias	
The Harry Potter wiki	harrypotter.wikia.com/wiki/Main_Page
Dinosaur wiki	iceage.wikia.com/wiki/Dinosaurs
Wiktionary (multilingual dictionary)	en.wiktionary.org/wiki/Wiktionary:Main_Page
Wikimedia	wikimedia.org.uk/wiki/Education
Some examples of critical thinking wikis	
Children's book reviews	childrensbookreviews.pbworks.com/w/page/15753294/FrontPage
Children's books wiki	childrensbooks.wikia.com/wiki/Children's_Books_Wiki
Example of a collaborative writing wiki	
Collaborative children's book writing wiki	Wikibooks en.wikibooks.org/wiki/Wikijunior

Table 6.3 (cont.)

Examples of primary school wikis	
Llanharan Primary School	llanharanps.wikispaces.com/
Moreland Primary School	56mps2013.wikispaces.com/
Example of a resource aggregator wiki	
The Student Room	www.thestudentroom.co.uk/wiki/ Useful_Teaching_Resources

Bloom's digital taxonomy *rubric* (Churches, 2009) provides one approach to assessing wiki editing within an educational context using the applying (which relates to authoring) and understanding (related to content) elements of Bloom's taxonomy, subdivided into four levels which may be useful for differentiating by outcome. Of course a practical issue you'll need to deal with is identifying and assessing individual contributions to the wiki. More broadly there is also the related issue of intellectual property and copyright as individual contributions to a wiki may be edited and modified by other contributors – so the question emerges as to ownership of the final product.

Wiki software and apps

Although specific software and apps are likely to change over a relatively short space of time, currently the well-designed MixedInk (www.mixedink.com) is a free educational Web 2.0 app that has great potential for Key Stage 1 and Key Stage 2 (NB the subscription version allows teachers to add password protection, pre-registration of pupils and activity reports). MixedInk supports a form of parallel or sequential construction where an initial piece of text is successively modified through remixing extracts of star rated contributions of the other authors in the group. The application usefully allows contributions of individual authors to be identified in the final remix.

Other Web 2.0 apps that have wiki features include Google Drive and Docs, ZoHo and the Blackboard VLE. (NB Remember to check the minimum age requirements, eg 13+ for a Google account.) Purpose designed software and online Web 2.0 tools for primary schools such as www.j2e.com are also worth considering though may require schools to pay annual subscription fees. Features of j2e are described at www.j2e.com/help/home2b/.

Critical questions

» *Explore the collaborative potential of MixedInk or Google Drive.*

» *How are opportunities for collaborative learning being supported by use of Web 2.0 internet apps at your school?*

Virtual worlds

Leander (2009) categorised responses to new media as *resistance* to new media; *replacement* which indicates a belief that traditional media will be replaced by the new media, eg the view that digital books may lead to a decline in printed books; *return* where the role of new media is regarded as supporting and enhancing engagement with traditional media; and *remediation* where the focus is on new media as mediating communication.

Resistance occurs where teachers regard new media as an unwelcome intrusion on established literacy practices though may also include the technophobic end of the technophobe/technophile dimension. For example, exploring the dialogue that commonly occurs in virtual worlds such as Second Life (www.secondlife.com) can lead to questioning educational value for primary pupils. Specifically for the primary school context My Tiny Planets (www.mytinyplanets.com) is an engaging experience which involves a range of interactive activities but again you'll need to plan how to get the most value from the synchronous chat area and recognise that there is open access to the site. Then again Club Penguin (www.clubpenguin.com) required activation via the child's parents' email address but the full package was quite expensive at £4.95 per month. On the other hand, the potential of virtual worlds for promoting authentic dialogue and communication within a school context was brought into focus by Merchant (2009) who evaluated a project involving primary school pupils in a virtual world called Barnsborough.

CASE STUDY

Barnsborough

> *Visitors to Barnsborough discover a world littered with evidence of human activity. Its previous inhabitants have simply vanished, leaving behind traces of their everyday lives in their notes, posters and journals. Phones are ringing and some have audio or text messages; computers have been left running; alarms are going; and vehicles simply abandoned.*
>
> (p 97)

The pupils used the evidence to generate ideas about what might have happened, eg people were abducted by aliens or some sort of eco disaster had occurred. The learning experience involved collaborative problem solving through use of a synchronous chat area and exposure to a variety of digital texts, eg signposts and *tool-tips* which when clicked provide helpful information and comments. The use of hyperlinks enabled pupils to access more extended text and multimedia, linked to national literacy objectives.

Comment

Pupils engaging with the Barnsborough experience found the virtual world that the teachers had created highly motivating. They referred to literacy activities such as note-taking, newspaper report writing and producing flashback stories as outcomes which suggests this was a very worthwhile experience though also suggests the *essentially printcentric (return)* perspective referred to by Leander (2009, p 148). In other words at least part of what was being valued was the traditional literacy activities that permeate the curriculum.

The *remediation* response is developed by Leander (2009) into a concept of *parallel pedagogy* which aims to make effective use of the affordances of new media rather than privileging one particular form such as the traditional printed text. This amounts to valuing multimodal texts, eg nuances of voice and facial expression can make a significant contribution to the communication of meaning. Arrangements of photos and other visual media can also help enrich the *voice* of the author. Children with different learning styles may also benefit from being given opportunities to present their work in a multimodal format. Digital literacy includes understanding the semiotics of the visual and moving image so children can be helped to improve their multimodal texts by learning the language of the visual image, eg significance of close-ups, mid-range and long shots, camera angles and elements of photo composition. A useful parallel to explore is the role of digital games, advocated by Marc Prensky (2007) as having a potentially transformatory role for teaching and learning within primary education.

Critical questions

» *Take a leap into the unknown and, if you haven't already done so, try out www. secondlife.com, www.activeworlds.com, My Tiny Planets and Club Penguin. What do you consider to be the educational potential of such virtual worlds?*

» *Multimodal texts extend the concept of reading, eg understanding the language of the visual image can help communicate more effectively. Think about use of different transition effects when linking video clips. Do different transition effects suggest different meanings? When might you use a* cross dissolve *rather than a* page peel?

Podcasting

The word *podcasting* is usually understood as a combination of iPod™ + broadcasting or as Playable On Demand + broadcasting (Barber and Cooper, 2012). In reality an iPod™ is not needed for podcasting as any device that plays MP3 files will serve the purpose, and that includes a wide range of devices. The *broadcasting* component is what separates a sound recording from a podcast (or where video is recorded, a *vidcast*). Podcasting itself is very simple and easy to do. A good place to start when looking for podcasts that others have created is by using an aggregator, also referred to as a pod catcher. An aggregator is simply a piece of software that maintains an up-to-date collection of podcasts in one convenient place. Typical aggregators are Juice and iTunes™, though Microsoft Outlook 2010 can also be used and folders can also be created within the web browser itself (a more extensive list is available at www.podcastdojo.com/podcast-managers-or-podcatcher/).

Podcasts and vidcasts are usually associated with RSS feeds (Really Simple Syndication). This is a fancy way of saying that it's possible to subscribe to a podcast, vidcast or web page so that the subscriber is immediately notified of any changes or additions. In Internet Explorer an orange icon is visible in the command bar when an RSS feed is detected on the page. When using Google's Chrome browser an extension needs to be installed such as *RSS Subscription Extension (by Google)*, *Foxish live RSS* or *RSS Feed Reader*.

The educational value of podcasting

As with other Web 2.0 tools such as blogs and wikis, podcasting helps to characterise the participatory web, the democratisation of the internet. The value of web 2.0 is recognised in Bloom's digital taxonomy (Churches, 2009), which places *creativity*, including use of Web 2.0 tools, at the top of the hierarchy. The downside of course is that the quality of the content of any particular podcast may be less than that of a professionally produced news item or documentary. It's also all the more important to develop critical evaluation skills to avoid being taken in by spoof podcasts just as with website counterparts and questionable wiki content. Nonetheless the list of worthwhile educational outcomes and outcomes specifically for pupils creating, publishing and listening to podcasts is extensive:

*   developing a *voice*;

*   producing content for an authentic audience;

*   providing a stimulus for discussion;

*   cross-curricular learning;

*   increased motivation and engagement;

*   developing speaking and listening;

*   supporting collaborative group work;

*   developing script writing;

*   helping to develop problem-solving strategies;

*   supporting different learning styles;

*   supporting assessment by enabling pupils to demonstrate their understanding rather than simply the end product;

*   developing IT capability;

*   support for communicating with parents.

Getting started

No sophisticated equipment is needed. Essentially all you need is a sound recording device, software for editing the audio/video and an internet connection; headphones are likely to be useful but there's no need for a separate recording area or recording studio. In fact, if children record their podcast in the classroom, the ambient noise can help create a newsroom atmosphere and interviewing in situ can convey authenticity when local sounds are included. Although a microphone plugged into a computer or laptop would be sufficient, or the computer's inbuilt microphone, you're likely to find a separate MP3 recording device such as Easi-Speak™ (available from www.tts-shopping.com) really useful – and these are already very popular within primary schools. Again, although it's possible to use a PC's basic sound recorder, multi-track audio recording and editing software is preferable. A typical podcast may include introductory and concluding music and may be compiled from several short clips and you'll find that multi-track recording and editing software is useful for this. *Audacity* (which is available as open source free software for different operating systems, eg Windows, Mac, GNU/Linux) is easy to use, is multi-track and includes a wide range of effects such as fade in, fade out, reverb, phaser, wahwah and many more. It's packaged with the Easi-Speak™ microphone but can also be downloaded for free from the audacity website audacity.sourceforge.net/ (NB After recording the podcast you need to export it as an MP3 file. *Audacity* requires that you install an extension file to enable exporting but the on screen instructions are very simple and only need a few mouse clicks). Other recording and editing software worth exploring for iPads™ include *Rap to Beats*, *Hokusai Audio Editor*, *Studio App Lite*, *Record Studio FREE*, *Studio. M* and *MultiTrack Song Recorder*.

Producing the podcast

Several quite similar models describe the process of producing a podcast from start to finish.

*   A straightforward approach uses the 5 p's: *Prepare, perform, produce, publish and promote*. This includes a focus on researching the topic, script writing and rehearsing (www.taglearning.com/by-publisher/softease/podium.html).

*   Fontichiaro (2011): (1) Picture it, (2) Plan it, (3) Record it, (4) Edit it, (5) Review it and (6) Distribute it. This model highlights revisiting earlier stages as need be, eg reviewing at stage five may lead directly to revisiting stage two if the overall effect was not as expected or to stage three if audio quality could be improved.

*   King and Gura (2007): the Podcast for Teachers (PFT) model includes a set-up phase and then a continuing phase which acknowledges that podcasts are typically produced as part of a series. The set-up phase includes – plan and *Create* the podcast, *Edit* in order to improve the recording, create a *Website* and upload the MP3 file, create the RSS and XML *Feed* and *Publish*. The continuing phase has the same structure but the website and RSS feed are edited rather than created. The sophistication of this two-phase model suggests it would be more suited to those with an interest in web page creation.

NB Websites such as www.podomatic.com essentially remove the need for creating web-pages and make publishing podcasts ultra-simple, though subscribers are encouraged to move from the free starter package to a monthly subscription fee. On the other hand web-sites such as www.blogger.com include aesthetically pleasing website templates, easy to follow instructions and analytics for monitoring all at no cost whatsoever.

Critical questions

»   *Locate some examples of podcasts created by primary school children either using a search engine or from the following direct link: www.sandaigprimary.co.uk/ radio_sandaig/index.php. What ideas do you get from listening to these for using podcasting in your own teaching?*

» *Reflect back on some recent teaching experience. Focus in particular on the medium term plans in one of the foundation subjects and identify how you might usefully incorporate podcasting.*

Other Web 2.0 tools

Similar to the wiki are tools which allow posting of messages, links and multimedia to a shared screen/wall. Using www.padlet.com you can set the privacy settings so that only those you give a password to can gain access and contribute to the wall. The Terms of Service specifically refer to schools using padlet.com with children under the age of 13 (jn.padlet.com/article/33-terms-of-service). Padlet is very easy to use and great for collaborative projects. Applications come readily to mind, eg a mind map produced during the whole-class teaching part of a lesson; children (and parents) might then access and add to the wall as part of a homework activity. Another application might be for posting suggestions on a topic of general interest that is reviewed as the term progresses.

Barber and Cooper (2012) include a useful review of a few of the many Web 2.0 applications that can be used in primary school classrooms including www.historypin.com, www.glogster.com, www.wordle.net, Twitter, Twitpic and TweetDeck. Finally, Classroom2.0 (www.classroom20.com/) is a social networking site for discussions related to all aspects of social media in education.

Critical question

» *Visit the Classroom2.0 social networking site and find a topic of interest relating to collaboration, communication and sharing. Identify relevant issues and discuss implications for developing the school's curriculum with others in your setting.*

Critical points

» *The chapter helped you to explore practical themes related to several key forms of Web 2.0.*

» *Questions were raised about the social meaning of blogging and the status of Wikipedia as a source of knowledge creation.*

» *The educational potential of blogging as an authentic learning experience was considered; the role of wikis to support collaborative learning was explored; and an inclusive approach to podcasting was suggested.*

» *You were encouraged to explore and evaluate the educational potential of some of the extensive range of Web 2.0 applications.*

Further reading and useful resources

For an interesting first-hand account of practical issues relating to a primary school blog started by a ten-year-old, read: Payne, M and Payne, D (2012) *Neverseconds: The Incredible Story of Martha Payne and How She Changed the World*. Glasgow: Cargo.

References

Barber, D and Cooper, L (2012) *Using New Web Tools in the Primary Classroom*. London: Routledge.

Boyd, D (2014) *It's Complicated: The Social Lives of Networked Teens*. London: Yale University Press.

Byron, T (2008) The Byron Report. [online] Available at: dera.ioe.ac.uk/7332/1/Final%20Report%20 Bookmarked.pdf (accessed 31 October 2014).

Carrington, V (2009) From Wikipedia to the Humble Classroom Wiki: Why We Should Pay Attention to Wikis, in Carrington, V and Robinson, M (eds) *Digital Literacies: Social Learning and Classroom Practices*. London: Sage, pp 65–81.

Chapman, C (2013) Complete Guide to Live Blogging. [online] Available at: www.hongkiat.com/blog/ complete-guide-to-live-blogging/ (accessed 31 October 2014).

Churches, A (2009) Bloom's Digital Taxonomy. [online] Available at: edorigami.wikispaces.com/file/ view/bloom's+Digital+taxonomy+v3.01.pdf (accessed 31 October 2014).

Fontichiaro, K (2011) Podcasting Tips. *Library Media Connection*, 29(5): 54.

King, K and Gura, M (2007) *Podcasting for Teachers*. Charlotte: Information Age Publishing Inc.

Leander, K (2009) Composing with Old and New Media: Toward a Parallel Pedagogy, in Carrington, V and Robinson, M (eds) *Digital Literacies: Social Learning and Classroom Practices*. London: Sage, pp 147–65.

McKenzie, J (2008) Beyond Cut-and-Paste. [online] Available at: fno.org/sept08/cut.html (accessed 31 October 2014).

Merchant, G (2009) Virtual Worlds in Real-Life Classrooms, in Carrington, V and Robinson, M (eds) *Digital Literacies: Social Learning and Classroom Practices*. London: Sage, pp 95–113.

Messer, A (2012) History Wikis. In Hayden, T (ed) *Using New Technologies to Enhance Teaching and Learning in History*. London: Routledge.

Miyake, N (2007) Computer Supported Collaborative Learning, in Andrews, R and Haythornthwaite, C (eds) *The Sage Handbook of E-Learning Research*. Los Angeles and London: Sage, pp 248–67.

Payne, M and Payne, D (2012) *Neverseconds: The Incredible Story of Martha Payne and How She Changed the World*. Glasgow: Cargo.

Prensky, M (2007) *Digital Game-Based Learning*. New York: Paragon House.

Rettberg, S (2012) All Together Now: Hypertext, Collective Narratives, and Online Collective Knowledge Communities, in Thomas, B and Page, RE (eds) *New Narratives: Stories and Storytelling in the Digital Age*. Lincoln: Bison, Ch 11.

Richardson, W (2009) *Blogs, Wikis, Podcasts, and Other Powerful Web Tools for Classrooms*, 2nd edition. Thousand Oaks: Corwin Press.

Shaffer, G (2012) Civility or Censorship? An Examination of the Reaction to a Proposed Code of Conduct for Bloggers, in *Blogging in the Global Society: Cultural, Political and Geographical Aspects*. Hershey: Information Science Reference, Ch 5.

Spring, M (1997) Collaborative Writing. [online] Available at: www.sis.pitt.edu/spring/cas/node31. html (accessed 31 October 2014).

Tapscott, D (2009) *Grown Up Digital*. London: McGraw Hill.

Tremayne, M (ed) (2007) *Blogging, Citizenship, and the Future of Media*. London: Routledge.

Watkins, C (2009) Easier Said than Done: Collaborative Learning. *School Leadership Today*, 1(1): 22–5.

West, J and West, M (2009) *Using Wikis for Online Collaboration: The Power of the Read-Write Web*. San Fransisco: Jossey-Bass.

7 Digital citizenship

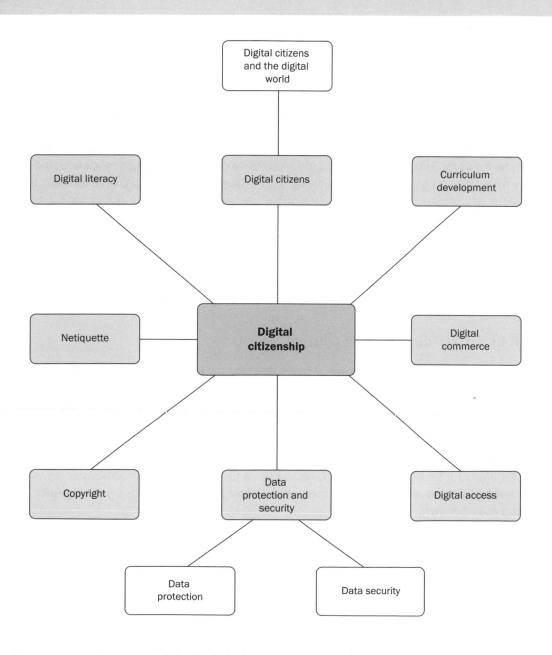

Introduction

Citizenship involves nationality and a sense of belonging or attachment to a particular country or state. Citizens typically have passports or identity cards to allow free movement and to confirm identity. These are particularly important documents in an uncertain world where individual freedom is valued and where personal identity is so essential to life as we know it. However, the concept of *digital citizenship* suggests the boundaries are not the physical boundaries of nations but the boundaries of digital technology. If the opportunity presents itself, watch the film *The Net* (1995), which provided a very vivid account of digital identity theft.

Digital citizens

Mossberger et al (2008) described a digital citizen as someone who uses the internet every day. An alternative way of describing digital citizens by Papacharissi (Webster, 2004) uses the term '*netizens*' which emphasises the character of the internet as a network of interconnections. But the emergence of Web 2.0 technology means that accessing the internet is now a more active and collaborative process and the website www.digizen.org refers to digital citizens as '*digizens*' in order to reflect this variety of participatory digital communication technology. The education of digital citizens involves developing confidence and capability with digital technology and the digital world. This includes a focus on e-safety, ethical behaviour and digital rights and responsibilities as part of character education aimed at developing good digital citizens.

Critical question

» *What does being a digital citizen mean to you? Do you see yourself as a* netizen *or a* digizen?

Digital citizens and the digital world

Understanding the digital world involves more than simply awareness of the internet and the various technological devices that provide access to the internet. Society in the twenty-first century is characterised more than ever before by technology enhanced mobility. It's not just the mobile phones that allow communication on the move but transportation in all its various forms also contributes to the sense of movement and change. And this movement is now faster and more continuous: messages sent via email arrive almost before they are sent, similarly for news flow via Twitter; Facebook is frequently used to communicate events as they happen; and rail and air links make movement between locations and countries easier than ever before.

The internet is part of the *Information Age* and the concept of knowledge explosion characteristic of the *Information Age* is well known. However, as Heppell (2011) notes, innovation in information and communication technology is already occurring at an exponential rate, so it may be more appropriate to refer to the *Digital Age*. The countless number of websites and multichannel TVs make for a more fragmented world. Globalisation involves both a decline of place as evidenced by McDonaldisation (Ritzer, 1983) and increasing diversity. The networked society of the post-industrial world comprises multinational corporations that outsource across national boundaries. We now live in a just-in-time society where the supply based economics of the past are being replaced by production to meet current needs. A job is no longer a job for life and facts learnt today may be out of date tomorrow. Acceptance of diversity, multitasking ability, self-reliance, critical awareness and entrepreneurial skills are just a few of the characteristics identified by Tapscott (2009) in *Grown Up Digital* when describing the character of the *screenagers*, the Net Generation, as better attuned to the new economy, networked society and digital world.

The anonymity of the internet is both an advantage and also a potential source of illusion. Communication is facilitated by anonymity as status differences are marginalised. But the internet is recognised as having a very long tail (Byron, 2008), which means that of the hundreds and thousands of websites only a very small percentage receive a high percentage of visits. The views of individuals as well as minority interest groups may therefore pass unnoticed. And even if politicians read contributions to newspaper blogs the political system has drifted a long way from the grassroots Athenian model of democracy. Message posters and bloggers may feel they have fulfilled some civic duty, and may feel empowered and active for having done so but how much difference is actually being made here?

Another characteristic of the internet is unregulated freedom of expression. This is both supportive of the democratic ideal of rational discussion and debate but also comes with a caveat emptor that appearances may be deceptive. Of course the internet is encompassed by a world imbued with capitalist ideology. And this is another area where *netizens* need to stay alert. It's common knowledge that news media are not politically neutral and also that commercial profit-seeking intrudes into all areas of life. Smartphones are even now beginning to alert shoppers to special offers as they pass along supermarket aisles and search engines are learning the browsing habits of potential consumers. Understanding *digital citizenship* involves understanding the nature of digital, the various guises of the internet and implications of digital technology within the broader context of the technological world and networked society of the Digital Age.

Critical questions

Reflect on aims of education appropriate for a rapidly changing world.

»   *What characteristics does a person need to be successful in this world?*

»   *What are the skills and character of a good digital citizen?*

»   *What are the characteristics of a good teacher in the digital world?*

Curriculum development

Ribble (2014) defines digital citizenship as the '*norms of appropriate, responsible behavior with regard to technology use*' and identifies nine key themes that are intuitively directly relevant to understanding digital citizenship. An alternative approach by Common Sense Media (CSM) is a comprehensive free resource for schools that divides the digital literacy component of the curriculum into three major strands: safety and security; digital citizenship; and research and information literacy. The digital citizenship strand is based on five units and the SWGfl has developed the CSM scheme for teaching digital literacy and citizenship in the UK using eight themes (Table 7.1).

Table 7.1 *Key themes*

Ribble (2014) Nine key themes	Common Sense Media (CSM) Planning and resources	SWGfl Linked to CSM
1. Digital Access 2. Digital Commerce 3. Digital Communication 4. Digital Literacy 5. Digital Etiquette 6. Digital Law 7. Digital Rights and Responsibilities 8. Digital Health and Wellness 9. Digital Security	1. Digital Life – this relates to the impact of digital media and what it means to be a responsible digital citizen 2. Privacy and Digital Footprints – this relates to personal information, both of self and others 3. Connected Culture – this relates to ethics including cyberbullying 4. Self-expression and Identity – this considers communicating through digital means 5. Respecting creative work – this relates to intellectual property rights	1. Internet Safety 2. Privacy and Security 3. Relationships and Communication 4. Cyberbullying 5. Digital Footprint and Reputation 6. Self Image and Identity 7. Information Literacy 8. Creative Credit and Copyright

Each of these themes is matched to a year group, linked to CSM lesson plans, resources and curriculum opportunities. For example, lesson 1 for Year 5 focuses on Privacy and Security. The lesson is called '*Strong Passwords*' and includes several online interactive resources to help set strong passwords. The identified curriculum opportunities for this lesson include brief descriptions of ICT and English links as well as an idea which suggests pupils use J2E to create an animation to give advice on passwords. All the materials are freely downloadable from www.digital-literacy.org.uk/. Taken as a whole these approaches provide comprehensive, detailed and accessible guidance and resources for teaching digital citizenship.

Critical question

» *The CSM lesson plans include lessons for each of the eight key themes. Choose one of the key themes as a starting point and consider how you would develop this theme progressively throughout the key stages. For example, CSM includes a lesson entitled Keep it Private in FS/Year 1, Powerful Passwords in Year 3, Private and Personal Information in Year 4 and so on through to Year 6. Can you identify the progression in these lessons?*

The following sections develop the key themes identified in Table 7.1.

Digital literacy

Although not separated into distinct sections, the national curriculum (DFE, 2013) includes content related to computer science, information technology and digital literacy. The focus on digital literacy includes developing criticality:

> For pupils (and teachers) to be digitally literate, they not only need to learn how to use technology in a variety of forms, but to be critical of information found electronically.
>
> (FutureLearn, 2014)

Sham websites help raise awareness of the need to be critical when accessing information online. The subheading of the website www.allaboutexplorers.com is 'Everything you've ever wanted to know about every explorer who ever lived ... and more!' However, the section on Christopher Columbus begins 'Christopher Columbus was born in 1951 in Sydney, Australia ...' and includes such details as 'Finally, the King and Queen of Spain called his toll-free number and agreed to help Columbus. In 1942 he set sail with three ships ...'.

There are plenty of sham websites to choose from and understandably it's not a recent phenomenon. Even the BBC has indulged when, for instance, in 2008 the iPlayer campaign was launched with a short video clip showing flying penguins. Search Google.co.uk for flying penguins bbc or read the full report at: www.brandrepublic.com/News/798436/BBC-launches-iPlayer-campaign-flying-penguin-footage/.

Teachers.tv resources relating to being critical of information stored digitally are still available and can be used as part of a cross-curricular approach to teaching. For example, the video news report relating to the proposal of the British Institute of Eating Control (BIEC) to introduce a £1000 fine if young people are caught eating certain banned foods helps challenge Key Stage 2 children to be critical of online sources (www.creativeeducation.co.uk/videos/watch-video.aspx?id=2975 and associated lesson plan resources www.proteachers-video.com/downloads/13844.pdf).

Is the tree octopus really an endangered species? The website (zapatopi.net/treeoctopus/) states that 'Tree octopuses became prized by the fashion industry as ornamental decorations for hats, leading greedy trappers to wipe out whole populations to feed the vanity of the fashionable rich'.

Sham websites draw attention to the need to teach children critical website evaluation skills. This topic is dealt with in Chapter 4, which focuses on information literacy, though you may find that the Cornell University resource is also useful for helping to identify evaluation criteria (olinuris.library.cornell.edu/ref/research/webcrit.html).

Critical question

Children might find it fun to create their own spoof website. Suitable software for creating webpages is included as part of the Web 2.0 tools designed for education available from www.j2e.com/lgfl.

» *What's your view about teaching children to create sham content as after all this could be seen as teaching them to be dishonest?*

Digital commerce

Related to the theme of biased, politically motivated or sham websites is the commercialisation of the internet that is intrinsic to capitalism. Web search engines are now able to learn users' browsing habits and target advertising accordingly. Advertising in itself can be informative but can also be intrusive. This is an important theme from the point of view of the Teachers' Standards related to '*the need to safeguard pupils' well-being*' (DFE, 2011). It may therefore be advisable, particularly in relation to children and those who are vulnerable, to install ad block software such as adblockplus which is freely downloadable and works with most browsers (adblockplus.org/). Parents should also be alerted to ways of dealing with unwanted advertising and online forms, where the required email address may subsequently be used for sending spam email. Other themes related to digital commerce relate to illegal downloading and online gambling.

Of course, advertising is potentially a worthwhile cross-curricular topic that can incorporate literacy, history, geography, design technology, art and information technology. Advertising provides a useful window into social history and culture, and provides opportunities for persuasive writing and design. However, you need to alert the pupils to the potential consequences of clicking on an online advert, such as exposure to viruses and spyware.

Web resources available for Key Stage 2 children include www.admongo.gov. This website includes an engaging online game aimed at raising awareness about advertising. Another useful web resource is Privacy Playground. This is an interactive story in a virtual environment in which the three cyberpigs encounter the perils of online advertising and spam emails (mediasmarts.ca/sites/default/files/games/privacy_playground/flash/privacy_playground_en/start.html).

The SWGfl scheme (www.digital-literacy.org.uk/) includes topics focusing on how the media promotes products for sale and also manipulates the perception of gender ('Things for Sale' in Year 3; 'Selling Stereotypes' in Year 6).

Critical question

» *Use the national curriculum programme of study to identify and reflect upon digital literacy learning objectives which would underpin a cross-curricular approach to teaching about advertising.*

Netiquette

Netiquette is a set of commonly agreed standards of conduct, or rules of communication that operate within the domains of cyberspace.

(Bell et al, 2004, p 114)

Netiquette, like etiquette, has a broad base of acceptable behaviour but within limits of variation. Non-compliance with rules of access can lead to being ejected and debarred from continued use of a website. Cyberspace is continuing to evolve so rules may also change. Consequently it can be useful to read terms and conditions of use when visiting websites. A simple instance is copyright in relation to digital images. Some images carry an explicit Creative Commons licence that allows users to copy and paste images provided the source is acknowledged; other images are subject to strict copyright. This is an area where you as the teacher can '*demonstrate consistently the positive attitudes, values and behaviour which are expected of pupils*' (DFE, 2011).

There are abundant websites, including school websites, which include lists of typical rules of conduct for children to follow. Such rules are underpinned by the need for avoiding misunderstandings, for integrity and by a digital interpretation of the Kantian categorical imperative: '*Do to others as you would expect them to do to you.*' In general, *Newbies* and *lurkers* may receive specific attention, eg develop some familiarity with the website before posting messages to the website's blog, don't ask too many questions and don't lurk in the background for too long either.

A typical list of netiquette for sending emails (adapted from Brusco, 2011) includes the following.

• In relation to clarity: use proper spelling and grammar because visual cues from facial expression and body language are absent. Similarly use of bullet points can aid clarity. Emoticons can be useful but they add a sense of informality so it's important to consider the audience. Capitalised words should be avoided as they suggest SHOUTING! The greeting can also suggest shades of formality which can also aid clarity.

• In relation to overuse: restrict use of the *High Priority* option to avoid becoming a boy who cried wolf. Similarly avoid too much use of *Reply All* as receiving irrelevant messages can be annoying for the recipient.

General rules of netiquette typically include rules such as: respect other users of the internet, don't engage in bullying behaviour and don't share private information. However, Heppell (2012) made the astute comment:

> *I've seen schools with 15 page Acceptable Use policies which just seem to me to miss the point completely. An Acceptable Use policy is only ever one sentence. It says, you know how we do things around here; online isn't any different ... bullying is bullying, rudeness is rudeness, inappropriate behaviour is ... online or face-to-face it doesn't matter. You know what the sanctions are, you know how we behave ... For school leaders to realise that the cyberworld is not any different to the face-to-face world is really very important.*
>
> (Heppell, 2012)

Nonetheless, although the sentiment is well founded, the freedom of the internet, which suggests anything and everything is possible, has the potential to be all-consuming and to sweep unsuspecting surfers from their surfboards. Specific and explicit teaching, the reminder that this is the real world too, is therefore vitally important. A good cross-curricular teaching opportunity would be for pupils to create a video to teach others about netiquette. A useful starting point would be to show the class the netiquette winning video 'Be Cool' by Mountfield School (2008) which illustrates excellent use of information technology as well as the pupils' engagement with rules of netiquette.

Critical question

Some acronyms are well known but use of acronyms might also mean that the received message is not understood, for example:

IOW that's really OTT but can talk about it next time. TIA, CUL – which in ordinary English translates as … In other words that's really over the top but we can talk about it next time. Thanks in advance, see you later.

» *Should you teach primary school children common abbreviations and acronyms? Explain your answer.*

Data protection and security

Data protection

The 1989 Data Protection Act (DPA) includes principles of data collection, rights of data subjects and complete and partial exemptions. Examples from the principles are that data must be kept up to date and can only be made available for registered purposes and users. An example of the rights of data subjects include the right to prevent distress, ie data subjects are entitled to prevent data being used in ways that would result in personal distress. On the other hand you're not entitled to have access to some personal data, eg police records and medical files; pupils are not entitled to access their school records and exam results prior to release; there is no entitlement to have access to employment references. An accessible source of information on the DPA is the BBC GCSE Bitesize ICT website (www.bbc.co.uk/schools/gcsebitesize/ict).

Data security

The Computer Misuse Act (1990) (CMA) identifies types of computer misuse such as hacking and the lesser offence of accessing someone else's computer files without permission; unauthorised copying of software; unauthorised copying, downloading and distributing of copyrighted material; abuse of email; illegal pornography; identity theft and viruses.

The topic of data security involves managing both physical and digital threats. Data can become corrupted through physical damage to the hard drive. Simple rules such as keeping liquids away from computers and making regular backups can avoid data loss. Anti-virus software is essential when computers are connected to the internet. Use of passwords can help avoid accidental deletion or modification of data by unauthorised users and is also a key consideration in staying safe online. The Information Commissioner website (ico.org.uk/) includes more detailed advice on keeping personal data safe with separate sections on computer, email, fax and staff training.

The SWGfl (www.digital-literacy.org.uk) scheme includes the related themes of Internet Safety and Privacy and Security. For example, the Year 4 lesson plan entitled '*Private and personal information*' together with a range of interactive resources such as Cyberquoll.

Critical question

» *With regard to your own school context, what impact does the approach to data security have on pupils' ability to locate relevant information when searching the internet? Consider alternative strategies.*

Copyright

The UK Copyright Service (UKCS) is a comprehensive source of information about copyright in the UK (www.copyrightservice.co.uk/copyright/). The website includes a focus on creators' rights, types of work, duration for different types of copyright, concept of fair use and permission. The topic of adding copyright to your own work is dealt with in a separate section on protecting your own work and includes a subsection on website copyright. Another area of particular interest when considering online sources is licensing your own work. This is considered as part of a *copyleft* topic and includes the Creative Commons licence.

According to the UKCS most countries have now signed up to the Berne Convention which established common copyright rights and protection in the international context. Following the Berne Convention all original work is automatically subject to copyright and this applies just as much to the internet as to literary and artistic works. Although not required by the Berne Convention, the UKCS advises that all online content, including webpages and images, include a copyright notice. The UKCS also provides useful advice on how to check for and deal with infringements of copyright.

The concept of fair use helps to support free speech, news reporting and educational use of copyright material. This is an area of copyright law where there may be some variation between different countries but what counts as acceptable fair use is generally similar. In the UK fair dealing is covered by the 1988 Copyright Designs and Patents Act (UK). As a general guide you can use copyrighted material without infringing copyright for non-commercial purposes such as private study, research, instruction, examination, criticism, review, news reporting, incidental inclusion and when supporting someone with a visual impairment. However, other conditions also apply, eg you're not allowed to make multiple copies when the purpose is research and private study; a reprographic process must not be used when copying material for instructional purposes (though check the Copyright Licensing Agency (schools.cla.co.uk)); the amount copied needs to be limited to what's required for criticism, review or news reporting. If you are planning to produce a derivative work including downloaded images or content from websites, the UKCS advises to check the copyright notice on the source websites and also to check that material on the websites is not infringing copyright. NB in relation to the internet, if a website is clearly intended to be used for educational purposes and doesn't include explicit restrictive copyright notices and if the website is being used by a teacher for educational purposes then the case for fair use will be strengthened. The general advice is to seek permission if there is any uncertainty.

Although automatic full copyright protects intellectual property it may not always be useful as it may sometimes be too restrictive. For example, if the intention is to share images or lesson plans that teachers may find useful then it would be better to make this purpose clear. The website www.creativecommons.org/ explains how to share work online by creating an appropriate Creative Commons licence. This is a simple and quick process. It's also free.

CASE STUDY

Copyright issues in Key Stage 2

Upper Key Stage 2 children can be introduced to copyright issues using simple role play scenarios.

Example: a group of Year 6 pupils are working on a class magazine project in geography related to places of interest. They have decided to focus on a particular town that has several interesting buildings and landmarks. They decide to use Google.co.uk to locate images as these will help bring their article to life. They soon locate many images but the best ones have a copyright symbol. What should they do?

Example: the group have decided to continue with the magazine project as a homework activity. While browsing the internet at home one of the pupils finds an educational website which aims to help children learn about architecture. The website contains lots of diagrams and images showing examples of different architectural features. One or two of these diagrams look like they might be useful for the magazine. Would it be OK to copy and paste these diagrams into an email and send it to another member of the group to help decide whether they are suitable?

Critical question

The Copyright Licensing Agency (schools.cla.co.uk) provides easy-to-access information about exceptions to copyright available for schools.

» *Enquire at your school whether you are allowed to make multiple photocopies of a text to support your teaching.*

Digital access

One of the broader encompassing themes of digital citizenship is the concept of digital access which relates to the broad aim of *'full electronic participation in society'* (Ribble, 2014). This is a social justice issue that brings the digital divide into focus as well as a political issue relating to national competitiveness on the world stage. Access to digital technology needs to be universal and approaches to addressing the digital divide need to focus on both availability of technology and capability. Several articles have explored the themes of parental engagement and home–school links in relation to reducing the digital divide, eg relating to the Home Access project, use of learning platforms and also policy implications (Davies and Jewitt, 2011).

Professor Stephen Heppell (2011) makes the interesting point that in the past pupils were *'banned from using the "new" ballpoint pens for fear that their cursive script handwriting might be ruined'*, and continued:

> *mobile phone technology is an integral part of very many classrooms: children summarise their understanding, snap images from the board, blog their field trips, bluetooth to their teachers, do day-in-the-life projects through their phones with other schools, sample and exchange data.*

Although this image may appear to relate more closely to older children, research evidence (Hollandsworth et al, 2011) suggests that 50–60 per cent of 10–11-year-old children use a mobile phone. This is part of what it means to be a digital citizen. However, Ohler (2012) emphasised the way in which schools may deny value to children's culture (the digital culture?) by requiring pupils to *'unplug when they enter school, and then plug back in again when they leave and re-enter the zone of continual connectivity that had no place during the school day'* (p 14).

Valuing children's culture means recognising and valuing choices and activities outside of school. Valuing the culture of family and parents also involves acknowledging different beliefs and lifestyles. Grant (2011) notes:

> *The creation of 'third spaces' where connections are forged between children's home and school funds of knowledge seems to promise a way forward that does not entirely erode boundaries, but enables children to connect and draw on resources from more than one cultural context.*

Critical question

» *Think about and write a brief summary on ways of drawing on these out-of-school expressions of culture that don't 'simply "transplant" elements from one domain to another' (p 300). NB Grant's article would be useful further reading.*

Kirklees Learning Service (2012) recognises that *'[primary] schools are beginning to incorporate [mobile phone devices], along with other mobile devices such as the ipad, ipod or tablet computers, into their curriculum'* (p 1). However, it is still early days and primary schools that do allow children to bring mobile phones to school typically do so only if pupils are making their own way to school unsupervised by an adult. There are many issues relating to use of mobile phones, eg cyberbullying, sexting, bypassing the school's filtered internet access and phoning home as soon as an incident occurs. A key point relating to the decision to allow or forbid mobile phones in school includes the need to have a clear policy and that both pupils and parents are aware of this. The Acceptable Use Policy (AUP) will need to contain a clear statement relating to use. Several primary schools have published their AUP on the internet, eg Decoy Community Primary School's Mobile Phone Policy was published in 2012 and includes *'We are happy [therefore] to allow pupils to bring their mobile phones to school provided that they follow a few simple guidelines'*. These guidelines, along with many schools, strictly forbid use of the phone in school though there are variations in the codes of conduct between schools, eg only Year 5 and 6 children may be allowed to bring their phones though are forbidden to use them once in school; Kirklees Learning Service (2012) identifies some alternatives ... if mobile phone use is permitted then the phone will only be used in lessons and then only with the agreement of the teacher and ... content must be shown to the teacher if requested. It's important to note that the potential issues relating to mobile phone use are very high on the agenda and that some AUPs go so far as to expressly forbid teachers from using mobile phones even for taking photos of children (Bishop Wilton CE Primary School, 2013); other AUPs allow teachers to take photos of children but only when accompanied by another member of staff and provided that this is recorded on an official form and wiped from the phone before leaving the school building (Heather Primary School, 2012).

Critical points

» *This chapter has raised questions about the meaning of digital citizenship and encouraged you to reflect on your own digital identity.*

» *There was a focus on the developing character of the internet in the Digital Age and the need to reflect on the aims of education in a rapidly changing digital world.*

» *Models of digital citizenship were identified in the context of the school curriculum and you were prompted to consider progression when planning to teach key themes.*

» *Digital literacy, commerce, data protection and security, copyright and access were considered in some detail. Look back at the key themes identified in Table 7.1 and explore the themes of* digital health and wellness *and* digital life.

Further reading and useful resources

Valuing children's culture and the third space helps to recognise the voice of the child.

• Professor Stephen Heppell presents a range of interesting perspectives on his heppell.tv blogspot that would be useful further reading (http://heppelltv.blogspot.co.uk/).

• A more direct focus on the concept of third space is included in the article by Grant, L (2011) 'I'm a completely different person at home': Using Digital Technologies to Connect Learning between Home and School. *Journal of Computer Assisted Learning*, 27: 292–302.

References

Addblockplus, adblockplus.org/ (accessed 31 October 2014).

Admongo, www.admongo.gov (accessed 31 October 2014).

Allaboutexplorers.com, www.allaboutexplorers.com (accessed 31 October 2014).

BBC Bitesize ICT, www.bbc.co.uk/schools/gcsebitesize/ict (accessed 31 October 2014).

Bell, D, Loader, B, Pleace, N and Schuler, D (2004) *Cyberculture: The Key Concepts*. London: Routledge.

BIEC, www.creativeeducation.co.uk/videos/watch-video.aspx?id=2975 (accessed 31 October 2014).

BIEC lesson plans, www.creativeeducation.co.uk/videos/watch-video.aspx?id=2975 (accessed 31 October 2014).

Bishop Wilton CE Primary School (2013) www.bishop-wilton-ps.org.uk/policies/cameras_&_phones_12.12.pdf (accessed 31 October 2014).

Brusco (2011) Tapping into Technology: Know your Netiquette. *AORN Journal*, 94(3): 279–86. [online] Available at: www.aornjournal.org/article/S0001-2092(11)00751-4/abstract (accessed 31 October 2014).

Byron, T (2008) The Byron Report. [online] Available at: dera.ioe.ac.uk/7332/1/Final%20Report%20Bookmarked.pdf (accessed 31 October 2014).

Common Sense Media, www.digital-literacy.org.uk (accessed 31 October 2014).

Creative Commons, www.creativecommons.org/about (accessed 31 October 2014).

CyberPigs, mediasmarts.ca/sites/default/files/games/privacy_playground/flash/privacy_playground_en/start.html (accessed 31 October 2014).

Davies, C and Jewitt, C (2011) Introduction to the Special Issue on Parental Engagement in Children's Uses of Technologies for Learning: Putting Policy into Practice in the Home. *Journal of Computer Assisted Learning*, 27(4): 289–91.

Decoy Community Primary School (2012) www.decoy.devon.sch.uk/Policies%202011%20-%202012/MOBILE%20PHONE%20POLICY%202012%20-%20E-Safety.pdf (accessed 31 October 2014).

Department for Education (2011) Teachers' Standards: Guidance for School Leaders, School Staff and Governing Bodies. [online] Available at: www.gov.uk/government/uploads/system/uploads/attachment_data/file/301107/Teachers__Standards.pdf (accessed 31 October 2014).

Department for Education (2013) The National Curriculum in England: Framework Document. [online] Available at: www.gov.uk/government/uploads/system/uploads/attachment_data/file/239033/PRIMARY_national_curriculum_-_Computing.pdf (accessed 31 October 2014).

Digizen.org, www.digizen.org (accessed 31 October 2014).

Earn digital passport online, www.commonsensemedia.org/educators/blog/announcing-new-ios-and-android-versions-for-the-award-winning-digital-passporttm (accessed 31 October 2014).

Flying penguins, www.brandrepublic.com/News/798436/BBC-launches-iPlayer-campaign-flying-penguin-footage/ (accessed 31 October 2014).

FutureLearn (2014) Teaching Computing Part 1, University of East Anglia, MOOC. [online] Available at: www.futurelearn.com (accessed 31 October 2014).

Grant, L (2011) 'I'm a completely different person at home': Using Digital Technologies to Connect Learning between Home and School. *Journal of Computer Assisted Learning*, 27(4): 292–302.

Heather Primary School (2012) www.thelifecloud.net/schools/HeatherPrimarySchool/spaces/Policies/ (accessed 31 October 2014).

Heppell, S (2011) workshop.heppell.mobi/search/label/mobile%20learning (accessed 31 October 2014).

Heppell, S (2012) www.youtube.com/watch?v=wFfateFgjmg&feature=youtu.be (accessed 31 October 2014).

Hollandsworth, R, Dowdy, L and Donovan, J (2011) Digital Citizenship in K-12: It Takes a Village. *TechTrends*, 55(4): 37–47. [online] Available at: link.springer.com/journal/11528 (accessed 31 October 2014).

Information Commissioner, ico.org.uk/ (accessed 31 October 2014).

J2e, www.j2e.com/lgfl (accessed 31 October 2014).

Kirklees Learning Service (2012) www2.kirklees.gov.uk/childrenandfamilies/teachersAndGovernors/pdf/mobile-phone-guidance-for-Primary-schools.pdf (accessed 31 October 2014).

Mossberger, K, Tolbert, C, McNeal, R and Ramona, S (2008) *Digital Citizenship: The Internet, Society, and Participation*. Cambridge, MA: MIT Press.

Mountfield School (2008) Be Cool. [online] Available at: www.youtube.com/watch?v=xVMq3G-JP04 (accessed 31 October 2014).

Net, The (1995) www.rottentomatoes.com/m/net/ (accessed 31 October 2014).

Ohler, J (2012) Digital Citizenship Means Character Education for the Digital Age. [online] Available at: www.eddigest.com (accessed 31 October 2014).

Ribble (2014) digitalcitizenship.net/Nine_Elements.html (accessed 31 October 2014).

Ritzer, G (1983) The McDonaldization of Society. *Journal of American Culture*, 6(1): 100–7. [online] Available at: http://s3-ap-southeast-2.amazonaws.com/jigsydney/general/PDF/271786~mcdonaldization.pdf (accessed 31 October 2014).

SWGfl, www.digital-literacy.org.uk/ (accessed 31 October 2014).

Tapscott, D (2009) *Grown Up Digital*. London: McGraw Hill.

Tree Octopus, zapatopi.net/treeoctopus/ (accessed 31 October 2014).

UK Copyright Service, www.copyrightservice.co.uk/copyright/ (accessed 31 October 2014).

Website evaluation, olinuris.library.cornell.edu/ref/research/webcrit.html (accessed 31 October 2014).

Webster, F (ed) (2004) *The Information Society Reader*. London: Routledge.

8 Digital identity and footprints for teachers

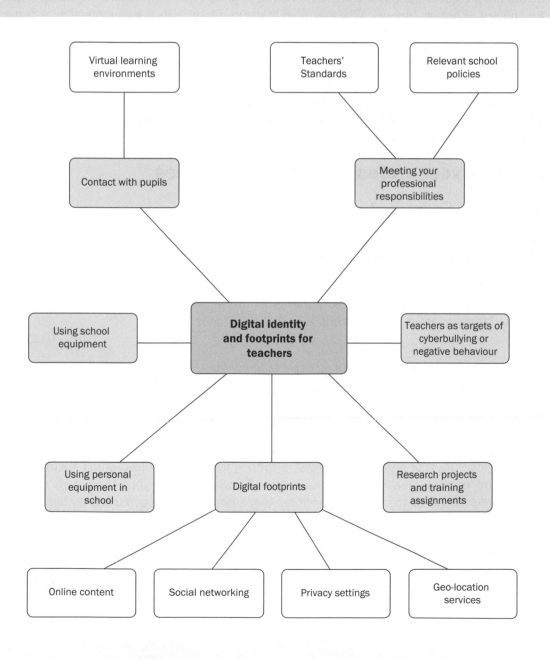

Introduction

As a trainee teacher you will probably already be making extensive use of technology, online services and content in your personal life and you now need to consider how this extends to your professional role. Technology, online services and content can offer rich rewards for professional development, teaching and networking but you need to be aware of some potential pitfalls and be in control of online content relating to you. As a professional your reputation is crucial and you need to ensure there is nothing that could damage the view training providers, schools, parents, colleagues and potential employers have of you. Similarly, you need to be able to protect yourself from others accessing your personal information or posting harmful content about you online. Now that both learning opportunities and professional duties are mediated by technology, often extending beyond school hours, the lines between the professional and personal may initially feel blurred. However, the Teachers' Standards are very clear that a professional level of conduct is expected within and outside of school (DfE, 2011). This chapter highlights aspects of your digital activities that need to be considered and offers some sensible ways to proceed to ensure your online professional reputation is safeguarded. A more detailed consideration of your professional role in relation to e-safety for pupils is given in Chapter 9.

Meeting your professional responsibilities

Teachers' Standards

Part two of the Teachers' Standards makes direct reference to your responsibilities in terms of personal and professional conduct:

> *A teacher is expected to demonstrate consistently high standards of personal and professional conduct ... Uphold public trust in the profession and maintain high standards of ethics and behaviour.*
>
> (DfE, 2011)

The following requirements refer to all aspects of conduct, however within this chapter they are interpreted in relation to technology and a teacher's digital identity.

As a trainee teacher you will be expected to demonstrate *'treating pupils with dignity, building relationships rooted in mutual respect, and at all times observing proper boundaries appropriate to a teachers' professional position'* (DfE, 2011). The appropriateness of having contact with children via social networks, texts, email, chat rooms, instant messaging and/or virtual learning environments (VLE), within and beyond the school day, will be explored. You need to be very clear about these boundaries to avoid any ambiguity that could be misinterpreted. You will also need to think through how you are going to explain your position to children who may send you, for example, friend requests on social networking sites.

Another important strand in the Teachers' Standards relates to *'having regard for the need to safeguard pupils' well being, in accordance with statutory provisions'* (DfE, 2011). Chapter 9 is dedicated to this vital topic and explores in detail your professional responsibilities in relation to e-safety education for children.

Teachers are also individuals with a variety of beliefs and opinions that may be voiced and discussed online. The Teachers' Standards state that you need to ensure '*that personal beliefs are not expressed in ways which exploit pupils' vulnerability or might lead them to break the law*' (DfE, 2011). Although this is an unlikely outcome you may wish to consider how you express yourself in online discussions on controversial topics if you are writing as an identifiable individual.

Explicit reference is made to the point that '*teachers must have proper and professional regard for the ethos, policies and practices of the school in which they teach*' (DfE, 2011). This also extends to the important principle of anonymity for the school, children, colleagues, parents and other members of that school community where you work if you are posting about your professional life anywhere online or via microblogging services such as Twitter. Being unfairly critical or disrespectful in online forums could have serious real-world consequences for your career.

Relevant school policies

Guidance on professional conduct in relation to digital technology and services may be contained in a number of policies. For example, e-safety and online conduct for staff and pupils will be detailed in each school's Acceptable Use Policy (AUP). Further, most schools will have a specific e-safety policy which explains the safeguarding measures you need to be aware of and the responsibility you have for e-safety education under the new national curriculum. Other generic documents you should be familiar with include the school's staff handbook that will cover what is expected of you in terms of your conduct and interactions with pupils. Similar information will also be included in your relevant Training Provider handbook. Each school should have clear anti-bullying and behaviour policies that apply to both pupils and staff and may be relevant in cases of cyberbullying.

Digital footprints

Up until now it may not have been important to consider your digital footprint and the impact this may have on your professional reputation. Any interactions you have online, content you have posted or content posted by others linked to your name, leaves a trail online. Over the years you may have created multiple online profiles which unless deleted are still available. Parents, colleagues, potential employers and training providers may conduct an online search for you and you need to feel confident that anything publicly accessible online complements your role in a position of trust educating children. On a cautionary note, even content you initially shared online only with friends could have been passed on to others or posted elsewhere. A simple rule to follow is that if it is something you would not be happy for your headteacher or a parent to see or hear, think very carefully before posting it online. This includes letting off steam about your day at school as a status update on your social network – the comments may come back to haunt you. The Open University offers this useful summary:

> *Your digital footprint is everything on the internet that is about you. This could include: a profile on Facebook or MySpace; photographs that you, your friends or family have posted online; anything you have written or that has been written about you, for instance on discussion boards, blogs, or in articles. We are all being encouraged to put aspects of ourselves and our lives online, and much of this content is freely available to view. Each time we add something about ourselves on the internet we enlarge our own digital footprint.*
>
> (Open University, 2014)

In addition to being aware of the risk to your professional reputation your digital footprint can have, it is also worth considering how your online presence can have a positive impact. The careers service at the Open University make some useful suggestions on how you can enhance your digital profile constructively (2014). *'Capitalise on your digital footprint'* by:

- *'Building a positive online presence that showcases your skills, experience and interests'*.

- Considering sharing an *'online profile that includes your CV, for instance on a professional networking site such as LinkedIn, can expand your range of contacts'*.

- Accessing *'professional networking sites'* (eg TES) *'connecting you to potential employers'*.

- *'Updating your profile regularly in a cost- and time-effective way'*.

- *'Carefully judged contributions to blogs, news articles and discussions, or by adding reviews to sites'*.

- *'Keeping a positive online presence regularly updated can reduce the impact of any earlier content you may regret, because most internet searches rarely access more than the top few results'* (Open University, 2014).

Online content

Your first step should be identifying what online content exists that directly relates to you. Reviewing and managing online content should now become a regular activity to ensure your professional reputation is protected.

Critical question

» *What online content exists linked to your name?*

  – *Carry out a search with your name.*

  – *Consider what impression of you these sources give in a professional context.*

Remember historical content may exist from old profiles that have not been deleted or posts from others that mention you.

Sources of online content can be varied and commonly include: social network profiles, photos and status updates (current and historical), microblogging, for example, tweets and retweets. From this point forward you should 'view managing your online reputation as an essential part of being a teacher' (Childnet International, 2011).

Social networking

Due to the prevalence of social networking in society it is worth spending some time exploring any potential tensions which might exist for teachers and what sensible precautions can be taken to protect your professional reputation.

Facebook

Critical question

» *Is it appropriate for trainee teacher Simon to accept a friend request on Facebook from two of his Year 6 pupils? Explain your answer in full, highlighting the issues raised.*

Whether to be friends with pupils on social networking sites has become a dilemma for many teachers, even in the primary setting, despite typical social networks requiring users to be 13 years old. The same question may be true of parents of pupils, including those you may already know, or prior pupils you have worked with. From a primary trainee teacher perspective one simple reason to decline online friendship requests is that the social networks do not advise use by those under 13 although, as the following chapter highlights, many primary-age pupils simply alter their date of birth in the registration process. Further, their membership may be without parental knowledge or consent. Childnet International (2011) commented that '*it is not a good idea to accept friend requests on your personal accounts or to accept requests to follow you (e.g. on Twitter) from pupils or even parents at your school*'.

Critical questions

» *Simon took the decision not to accept the friend requests but then felt awkward when the children in question approached him in person at school to ask again. How should Simon explain his response to the pupils?*

» *Further, how should he address the issue of children having profiles on social networks when they are underage? Does he have a responsibility to inform parents?*

Most children will understand if you explain you use some online services when you are being a teacher, for example the school's VLE, and others when you are at home with your friends and family, for example Facebook. This is similar to how you would explain that at school people use your title and surname but your friends and family use your Christian name. Children may be curious about your Christian name but are then happy that it is not appropriate to use it in the school context.

When it comes to adults, including parents and colleagues, that you do not want to accept requests from, it is useful to know that with most services the person is not informed if you decline, ignore a request or even delete a person from your friends/subscriber list.

Childnet International (2011) clarifies the reasons for being cautious:

> *by accepting such requests you could be making yourself vulnerable by sharing personal information or by having access to personal information about your pupils. You may be potentially leaving yourself open to allegations of inappropriate contact or conduct or even find yourself exposed to unwanted contact.*

These points directly relate to the Teachers' Standards requirement to maintain appropriate professional boundaries with children. However innocent and well intentioned, you need to think carefully about how these communications could be misinterpreted. Effective teaching requires clear teacher–pupil boundaries and there are usually organisational alternatives. For example, school email addresses and discussion boards on the school's VLE/MLE that reinforce these boundaries can be conducive to extending learning and teaching opportunities. Most teaching unions also advise limiting contact online with pupils to school-based systems; for example, the school's VLE/MLE, a clearly defined space for educational purposes.

As discussed it is not recommended that you are in contact with pupils via personal social networking accounts; however, should you come across material of concern relating to a pupil you know, you have a professional responsibility to report it directly to the named safeguarding person identified at the school.

A further point to consider is who you have on your friend, follower or contact lists. Childnet International (2011) recommends that you:

> *think carefully about whom you are friends with, and which friends can access what information. It is a good idea to remove any friends or customise the privacy settings for current friends, if access to your personal activity could compromise your position, for example parents with children at school.*

Always think before you post as there is the possibility that friends could re-post what you have written and you no longer have any control of that content.

In summary, Childnet International (2011) recommends these steps to protect your online reputation.

- *'Always think carefully before making any posts, status updates or having discussions regarding the school, its staff, pupils or parents in an online environment – even if your account is private. Comments made public could be taken out of context and could be very damaging. Think about the language you use – abrupt or inappropriate comments, even if they were made in jest, may lead to complaints'.*

- *'Posting derogatory comments about pupils, parents or colleagues is never acceptable and potentially could have serious consequences in terms of employment or legally by bringing your school or profession into disrepute'.*

- Be mindful in choosing a profile image or pages you like to be confident you are presenting yourself how you would like to.

- Deactivate old accounts and delete old material regularly.

Using social networking for educational purposes

Critical question

» *Rasina would like to use Facebook as a tool for a class project over the holiday period. What issues should she consider before undertaking this activity?*

As new forms of online services continue to evolve this distinction between personal and professional needs to be discussed and revisited regularly. It would be a shame to blanket all technologies and online services together and not use their potential for learning and teaching. It is recommend that you always consider the primary purpose and use to inform your adoption decisions. Within some educational establishments social networking services are automatically blocked. With older learners many educators are exploring using Facebook and other social networking services with some success; however, this is not normally with personal accounts. If you would like to utilise the functionality of some of these services; for example, email, chat rooms, collaborative wikis, etc, explore what tools are available in online learning tools and services provided by the organisation you are working in.

> *Some educators and schools do use Facebook or other SNS to connect and communicate with pupils, parents, and governors, but they do so using professional or organisational accounts or pages, with prior approval from their Senior Leadership team and recognising that Facebook and many SNS do have a minimum age requirement of 13.*
>
> (Childnet International, 2011)

Microblogging: Twitter

Twitter is increasingly being used educationally in subject-specific disciplines to highlight key thinkers or leaders worth following. Similarly, following key commentators, to be informed about professional discussions taking place, can be a very useful way to keep up-to-date with national policy changes or educational debates. Protecting your professional reputation does not mean you cannot express an opinion in professional and public spaces but that you do so in a manner conscious of your role and potential audience. Consider whether what you have written is appropriate for anyone who knows you in a professional context to read without causing offence or damaging your professional reputation. Not using an obvious user name or email address might offer further privacy, as these are the common ways to search for users. This is not necessarily being surreptitious but drawing a distinction between your professional and personal identities.

Privacy settings

It is crucial that you have a comprehensive understanding of privacy settings on any online services that you use to protect your personal information. Privacy settings can often be set individually for viewing posts and status updates, photos, videos, timelines and other personal information. It is important to remember you do not have access to control the privacy of things you write on another person's wall or page. Specific advice for Facebook is available at www.facebook.com/help/445588775451827 and for Twitter at support.

twitter.com/articles/14016-about-public-and-protected-tweets. Privacy setting protocols regularly change or are updated so you need to establish the habit of checking these regularly.

Geo-location services

If you are using a 3G or 4G tablet or a smartphone you may well be using geo-location services. This is where your location can be pinpointed in time often through a third party application. Sometimes the default setting can be on, or it is easy to unintentionally allow access when hurrying through set-up processes. The device's signal is used to map location in time and space. In learning contexts, for example, on a geography fieldtrip, generic geo-location functionality may have real learning potential; however, you may not want places you visit in your personal life to be publicly shared. Again these can often be made private and only accessible to friends or customised further to specific individuals.

Using school equipment

Many schools endeavour to encourage teachers to embrace technology by allowing them to take school laptops or tablets home for professional duties. Several important considerations additionally apply. If you are accessing personal accounts or websites on school devices, first be sure you are happy for these to be available in the computer history and that they are not in breach of staff guidelines. Second, it is not recommended that you use the 'save password' options as this could mean subsequent users, staff or children, would have access to your personal information.

School devices may contain a wealth of information about pupils or the school and you need to be aware that whilst the device is in your possession away from the school premises you are responsible for ensuring the data remains secure and is not accessed by any unauthorised persons. Digital safeguarding is explored further in Chapter 9 on e-safety, as potential risks exist if this information becomes public in any way. Staff guidance and Ofsted inspection criteria directly address this important safeguarding issue.

If you are logging on to personal accounts and online services using a school laptop it is recommended that you do not use the save password option as this could lead to subsequent users gaining automatic access to personal information available on these accounts. Ensure you always manually logout of any online services as not all have default logout options after set time periods and you shouldn't rely on this safeguarding feature alone. If you have previously used the save password option you will need to delete the cookies to remove the saved passwords. For privacy you may also want to delete the browsing history as this may take subsequent users to web pages you have visited, including login pages for online services. Some school policies may prohibit personal use and recommend that the laptop or tablet is only used directly for professional duties such as lesson planning, report writing and assessment. Obviously it is not recommended that you store personal photographs, videos and music on school-owned devices. Housekeeping and deleting personal files should be undertaken regularly. You wouldn't want your pupils to read your last letter to the bank manager for example. It is possible to set up multiple password-protected user accounts on devices that would offer some level of protection as long as you have set a strong password. It is worth noting that the registered administrator on the device can often override user account settings.

Using personal equipment in school

Most teachers will have access to a range of digital devices that can capture and store information, access online content and share data via online services. These are likely to include mobile phones, especially smartphones, laptops, PCs, tablets, digital cameras and portable storage devices. Increasingly these are portable and WiFi enabled, meaning it is often convenient both to bring them into school and utilise them for professional duties. Without limiting the potential positive contribution these devices can make, there a few basic considerations to undertake. Consider carefully what data is stored locally on your computer that you do not want others to routinely access.

Personal devices such as smartphones, iPads and tablets should ideally be stored securely on school premises and have PIN protection set up on initiation screens to prevent others accessing your personal information. When passwords are required, ensure they are secure and not easy to guess. A recent survey highlighted that a large percentage of people use the passwords '*password*' or '*1234*'; obviously these are not very secure. One recommended formula is to use a mixture of lower and upper-case letters, numbers and symbols.

Critical question

»   *Gemma, a trainee teacher, is accompanying her class on a two-day residential trip to Sherwood Forest. She plans to take her digital camera to capture elements of the trip to share with the children when they are back in the classroom as part of their personal learning logs. Explain which issues Gemma should consider before proceeding.*

If a school or organisation digital camera is available it is recommended that teachers use that in preference over personal devices, as images of children will be taken and stored. If it is necessary for you to use a personal device you should transfer the images onto school equipment as soon as possible and then delete them from your own device. Whilst the images or recordings are held on a personal device you are responsible for ensuring the data is kept safe and secure at all times. Before any images are taken you also need to consult school protocols relating to parental consent, purpose, storage and publication. You must follow the school protocols precisely as these will have been agreed by the senior management team and shared with parents when consent was sought. This also applies to publishing images obtained of children or staff and precise local guidance will be in place and you should seek clarity from your school. As a general principle you should not publish images or videos on any publicly accessible forum without specific consent from parents in advance as there are a number of safeguarding issues.

Teachers as targets of cyberbullying or negative behaviour

The Department for Children, Schools and Families (DCSF) defined cyberbullying as *'the use of Information and Communications Technology (ICT), particularly mobile phones and the internet, deliberately to upset someone else'* (DCSF and Childnet International, 2009). Further:

> *Cyberbullying may consist of threats, harassment, embarrassment, humiliation, defamation or impersonation. Cyberbullying may take the form of general insults, or prejudice-based bullying, for example homophobic, sexist, racist or other forms of discrimination.*

> *There have been cases of school employees being cyber bullied by current or ex-pupils; by colleagues, parents and other adults; and by people who attempt to remain anonymous.*

> *There are reported cases of cyberbullying involving email, VLEs, chat rooms, web sites, social networking sites, mobile and fixed-point phones, digital cameras, games and virtual world sites.*

> (DCSF and Childnet International, 2009)

How extensive is the problem of cyberbullying amongst school staff?

- *'15% of teachers responding to a 2009 survey carried out by Teacher Support Network and The Association of Teachers and Lecturers reported they had been victims of cyberbullying'* (cited in DCSF and Childnet International, 2009).

- 46 per cent of teachers surveyed for Becta's E-Safety and Web 2.0 Report (September 2008) reported negative experiences caused by pupils using Web 2.0 technologies (defined as participatory mobile and web-based sites and services) (cited in DCSF and Childnet International, 2009).

- In May 2007 the NASUWT surveyed teachers over a period of five days on cyberbullying. Almost 100 teachers reported incidents of cyberbullying by pupils using mobile phones and web-based sites that had caused real distress and trauma (cited in DCSF and Childnet International, 2009).

Critical question

» *Nathan, a trainee teacher, received derogatory comments about one of his lessons posted on his Facebook wall by a user not known to him. He finds this troubling and is tempted to search for further references to himself on websites he has heard the children mention; for example, ratemyteacher. What would you advise him to do and why?*

Unfortunately there are instances of teachers being the target of malicious or disrespectful online posts. Childnet International (2011) suggested a number of steps you can take should this happen to you.

- If you have been tagged in a photo you do not wish to be seen you can often untag yourself. Additionally politely request that the photo you are in is taken down or at least made private.

- Should the content breach a social networking service's terms of use you can report it directly.

- Save or print out copies of posts, messages or images that you find abusive as evidence.

- Generally it is advisable not to respond directly.

- Report and seek advice from the senior management team at your school.

At times it might be hard to distinguish when something is crossing a line and becomes offensive. Children have always talked about teachers, both positively and negatively, and this won't change. However, with today's applications a trail is left. As a general principle don't actively go looking for comments, but obviously if they are particularly upsetting or targeted directly at you on social media you have a justifiable cause of complaint. Remember your training provider and/or school also has a duty of care with regards to your health and well-being and they should have protocols in place to deal with such instances.

DCSF states:

> All employers including employers of school staff have various statutory and common law duties to look after the physical and mental health of their employees. Protecting staff from cyberbullying is best done within a prevention framework, with whole school policies and practices designed to combat cyberbullying. Each school should have a designated cyberbullying lead, a member of the senior management team tasked with overseeing and managing the recording, investigation and resolution of all bullying incidents.
>
> (DCSF and Childnet International, 2009)

Contact with pupils

Critical question

Ahmed wants a quick and effective way to communicate and engage with his Year 5 pupils about their homework and is thinking of giving them either his mobile number or email address as they seem very keen to use technology in their learning and most have access to the internet via smartphones or similar mobile devices.

» *Should he go ahead with these plans or can you think of alternative approaches that may be equally as effective in engaging learners?*

Virtual learning environments

Many schools, including primaries, subscribe to VLEs or MLEs to utilise in learning and teaching within and beyond the school premises and day.

A virtual learning environment (VLE), or learning platform, is an e-learning education system based on the web that models conventional in-person education by providing equivalent virtual access to classes, class content, tests, homework, grades, assessments, and other external resources such as academic or museum website links. It is also a social space where students and teacher can interact through threaded discussions or chat. It typically uses Web 2.0 tools for 2-way interaction, and includes a content management system.

(Wikipedia, 2014)

Typical functionality includes:

- *content management – creation, storage, access to and use of learning resources*

- *curriculum mapping and planning – lesson planning, assessment and personalisation of the learning experience*

  - *learner engagement and administration – managed access to learner information and resources and tracking of progress and achievement*

  - *communication and collaboration – emails, notices, chat, wikis, blogs.*

(Wikipedia, 2014)

A VLE will have a cost implication, especially if an external server or hosted solution is used, so adoption will be a whole school or cluster decision. The advantages will be school designated user names and access with tracking data.

Example primary VLEs you may wish to explore include:

- StudyWiz Primary (www.apac.studywiz.com/?page_id=119).

- Uniservity (www.uniservity.com).

- Frog Primary Learning Platform (www.exa.net.uk/education/virtual%20learning%20platform).

Research projects and training assignments

Often trainee teachers are asked to carry out classroom research or to reflect on their professional experiences on placements in coursework, including portfolios and assignments. This also applies to serving teachers involved in continued professional development with external parties. Careful thought is needed to ensure you are not in breach of school protocols. Some schools may impose a blanket ban on collecting research data on children whilst others will agree with certain provisos in place following a detailed discussion.

Critical question

» *In addition to using the digital photographs from the school residential trip to Sherwood Forest Gemma plans to use some of the images in a university assignment on the benefits of outdoor learning. What should Gemma consider before proceeding?*

On all occasions reference to school-based experiences in external documents of any form must be anonymous to respect individual privacy. The school or organisation, children, staff and parents must not be identifiable even if you are being complimentary rather than giving a professional critique. If the scope of what you intend using digitally captured data for goes beyond the scope or remit of what the school has agreed with parents, specific parental consent must be sought. If in doubt seek parental consent in writing. It is very important to always pixelate faces and remove identifying features such as school logos, and of course, do not include names. Remember this principle also applies to appendix material. In your consent form explain carefully the purpose of your project, what data will be captured, how it will be stored, whether it will only be used in the analysis stage or form part of the final publication, who will have access to the data and when it will be destroyed. Often parents will agree when they have a full picture of the process and professional reassurances have been made.

Critical action points

» Review and update any online content relating to you to ensure your professional reputation remains positive.

» Carefully consider the distinction between your personal and professional life in relation to contact with pupils, social networking and use of equipment.

» Consult relevant school policies and ensure you do not breach these.

» Be proactive in ensuring your online privacy and be aware of cyberbullying advice.

Table 8.1 Auditing your digital footprint

Recommended tasks	Tick when complete	Notes/further action needed
Search for your name on the internet (you may want to extend this to include your nicknames/usernames)		
Delete any out of date/no longer used profiles		
Consider setting up an alert system for your name, eg Google alerts (see: www.google.co.uk/alerts)		
Check and update the privacy settings for all your online profiles and postings		
Consider joining professional social networking sites (you will need to keep these up to date)		

Further reading and useful resources

A useful range of presentations on the topic of digital footprints can be found at: cybraryman.com/digitalfootprints.html.

Teachers and Technology: a checklist for trainees and NQTs expands upon points raised in this chapter and can be found at: www.childnet.com/downloads/Teachers-and-technology.pdf.

If you do become the target for cyberbullying this excellent resource gives very good advice on how to deal with it and relevant contact information: www.digizen.org/downloads/cyberbullying_teachers.pdf.

References

Childnet International (2011) *Social Networking: A Guide for Trainee Teachers and NQTs*.

Department for Children, Schools and Families and Childnet International (2009) Cyberbullying: Supporting School Staff. [online] Available at: www.digizen.org/downloads/cyberbullying_teachers.pdf (accessed 31 October 2014).

Department for Education (2011) Teachers' Standards Guidance for School Leaders, School Staff and Governing Bodies. [online] Available at: www.gov.uk/government/uploads/system/uploads/attachment_data/file/301107/Teachers__Standards.pdf (accessed 31 October 2014).

Facebook (2014) Privacy. [online] Available at: www.facebook.com/help/445588775451827 (accessed 31 October 2014).

Open University (2014) Digital Footprints. [online] Available at: www2.open.ac.uk/students/careers/job-seeking/digital-footprint (accessed 31 October 2014).

Twitter (2014) Public and Protected Tweets. [online] Available at: support.twitter.com/articles/14016-about-public-and-protected-tweets (accessed 31 October 2014).

Wikipedia (2014) Virtual Learning Environments. [online] Available at: en.wikipedia.org/wiki/Virtual_learning_environment (accessed 31 October 2014).

9 E-safety and digital safeguarding

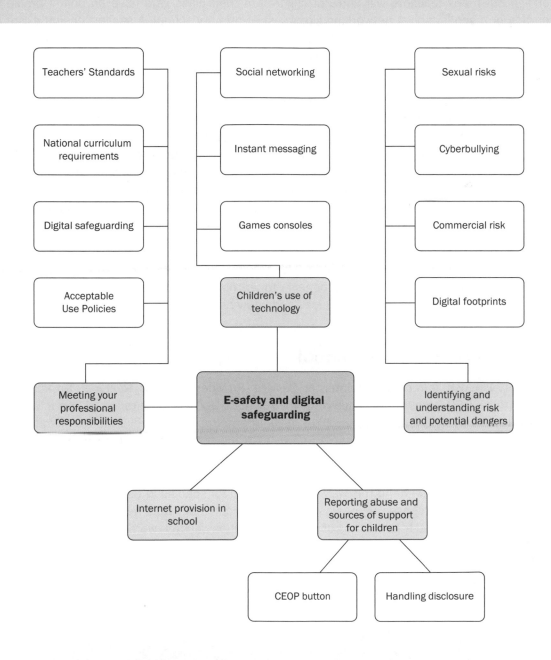

Introduction

As a trainee or practising primary teacher the area of e-safety is challenging, evolving and complex. You will need to be aware of the vast range of technologies and online services children of primary age are using. These technologies change with trends and often have functional features that can create potential risks. How the profession and you as a trainee respond in terms of e-safety education requires careful consideration of a number of aspects; for example, balancing of risk and the need to inform and educate in relation to children's ages. Many aspects are problematic, for example, Facebook requires users to be 13 years of age but many teachers will know of children in their class who have an online profile on this or a similar social networking site whilst at primary school. A similar tension exists when considering how filtered access to the internet is within school compared to potentially open access at home. Your role may extend to educating parents about e-safety alongside children.

The first step in preparing yourself as a professional is to understand your responsibilities in relation to e-safety in terms of the Teachers' Standards and requirements of the computing programmes of study that come into place in September 2014. Your school setting will have policies and protocols that it is essential for you to locate and understand. Each school will have several policy documents including an Acceptable Use Policy relating to staff and pupil use of the internet on school premises, protocols for safeguarding pupil data and handling disclosures made by children. Always ensure you act in accordance with the agreed policies at the school you are working in and be aware that these may vary between your placement schools.

When you embark on e-safety education with children, preparation is essential. You need to be familiar with the technologies, benefits to learning, potential risks, be able to locate age-appropriate tried and tested resources and know how to handle a disclosure should this arise.

Internet provision in school

Schools will use a recognised Internet Service Provider (ISP) or Regional Broadband Consortium (RBC) to purchase access for their school; age-related filtering will be in place which is actively monitored (Ofsted, 2014, p 8). Internet access has evolved over time with many schools moving towards what is known as a managed system. Initially there was a temptation for schools to have locked down systems that were highly filtered and sanitised versions of the internet; sometimes sites could only be accessed if they had been unblocked one by one. On the one hand this was very reassuring for schools in terms of e-safety, however; one unforeseen consequence was that many educationally valid websites were blocked. Similarly, it was argued that in terms of e-safety education children were not being presented with a realistic experience similar to what they would face at home and this approach could in fact be putting children at greater risk. Hence, there has been a shift towards managed systems, negating some of the risks of accessing inappropriate material, and highlighting the importance of empowering children to understand risks and how to keep themselves safe. Ofsted reported that:

Pupils in the schools that had 'managed' systems had better knowledge and understanding of how to stay safe than those in schools with 'locked down' systems. Pupils were more vulnerable overall when schools used locked down systems because they were not given enough opportunities to learn how to assess and manage risk for themselves.

(2014, p 4)

Meeting your professional responsibilities

In order to meet your professional responsibilities you need a clear understanding of: your role as detailed by the Teachers' Standards, the new national curriculum requirements, digital safeguarding protocols and key policy documents, for example, a school's Acceptable Use Policy.

Teachers' Standards

Ofsted detail a school's e-safety responsibilities as '*to protect and educate pupils and staff in their use of technology*' and '*to have the appropriate mechanisms to intervene and support any incident where appropriate*' (2014, p 4). This underscores the principle that e-safety protocols and e-safety education is a responsibility of all trainees, teachers and adults working in a school and not just the computing subject leader or the domain of discrete computing sessions. Ofsted will look for a whole-school consistent approach (2014, p 8). Nor should you view e-safety education as a one-off topic, it should be an on-going process throughout Key Stages 1 and 2 and visited regularly, for example, via assemblies, pastoral time, personal, social and health education lessons (Ofsted, 2014, p 4). Technology is used across the curriculum and often class teachers are best placed to handle issues that are potentially sensitive with their learners as they know them best. As a trainee you should always talk with your class teacher about any plans you have for including e-safety aspects in your teaching. You will need to know about experiences they have had to date, whether there are any child protection issues or additional sensitivity required. Even when using well-established educational materials which are categorised by age you need to ensure you have viewed the materials in full in advance and discussed any concerns with your class teacher. You should be aware that access to technology and the internet can vary widely at home for the children in your care. Hopefully your plans will complement plans already in place at your school although you should be prepared to respond to queries or concerns as they arise. As soon as you begin visiting a new school placement ask to see the e-safety policy documents to ensure you are clear about the school's expectations of your professional conduct in relation to e-safety and safeguarding more generally. It would also be worth enquiring about any staff training opportunities whilst you are on placement and whether any parent education sessions are planned that you could attend whilst training at the school.

Your overarching aim should be to empower children to keep themselves safe by helping them to understand the benefits and risks involved with technology in a balanced and factually accurate way. Be truthful but not scaremongering and ensure there is always time for children to discuss and question both you and their peers. You should remember to include discussing the benefits to learning and leisure technology can bring and maintain perspective on the dangers and risks. The goal is not to terrify or dissuade children from using technology but to enable them to make informed choices and manage risk. The Teachers' Standards, under which you must operate, make reference to *'having regard for the need to safeguard pupils' wellbeing'* with respect to personal and professional conduct (DfE, 2011, p 10). A teacher's subject knowledge is crucial and again this is echoed in the Teachers' Standards in relation to having a secure knowledge of curriculum areas, keeping up to date and having a critical understanding of developments (DfE, 2011, p 7). Ultimately during training and post qualification these are your legal obligations as a professional. Keeping up to date requires career long continuing professional development and ideally this area of your expertise should be visited annually as technology and trends evolve. Ofsted has been critical about the *'extent and quality of training for staff in schools'*, specifically that it is often not systematic and the impact is not comprehensively monitored (2014, p 5). As this is such a crucial area you are strongly recommended to make the most of your school training by undertaking your own professional development activities starting with some of the resources suggested in this chapter.

National curriculum requirements

E-safety has been a priority area in primary education for several years and many professionals welcomed the explicit statements that have been included in the national curriculum 2014 programmes of study for computing. At Key Stage 1 pupils should be taught to: *'use technology safely and respectfully, keeping personal information private; know where to go for help and support when they have concerns about material on the internet'* (DfE, 2013, p 189). Further at Key Stage 2 pupils should be taught to *'use technology safely, respectfully and responsibly; know a range of ways to report concerns and inappropriate behaviour'* (DfE, 2013, p 189). It is crucial that you listen to the children in your care, their experiences and views as this will help ensure your e-safety education is relevant and will have impact. Data is available for national trends but within a locality, school, class or sub-group particular software applications may well be favoured over others. Favourite websites spread quickly amongst groups as there is a natural tendency for children wanting to conform and fit in with their peers.

In summary, for you to be able to teach the e-safety components specified in the national curriculum, you must:

- be able to identify the technologies the children you are working with are typically using both at school and at home;

- have a good understanding of the functionality of these technologies and applications even if it is your preference not to use them personally in your professional or personal life;

- understand privacy settings and the notion of leaving a digital footprint when any data is shared online;

- be aware of the benefits and potential risks inherent in these technologies;

- be aware of how concerns can be reported as both a professional and as a child;

- be aware of netiquette, responsible and respectful online protocols and be able to model and communicate these to learners;

- have a mechanism, personally and within the school context, for keeping up to date.

Critical questions

» *How prepared are you to teach the e-safety components of the computing programmes of study listed above?*

» *Identify any knowledge gaps you currently may have. Use this chapter and the suggested further reading and resources to ensure you have a sound grasp of the key areas listed.*

Digital safeguarding

You should be aware of legal and school based procedures for the digital safeguarding of pupil data. You need to know how to legally and appropriately access, update, store and retrieve any digital data that identifies personal information about the children in your care both on and off school premises. Ofsted highlights the key area of management of personal data in inspection guidance based on the Data Protection Act 1998. Inadequate practice is detailed as where personal data is unsecured or not encrypted, especially if taken from the school site (2014, pp 8–9). Whilst there is a responsibility on schools to have clear protocols in place and ensure all staff are aware, as a visiting trainee you are recommended to make direct enquiries about what is permissible or not. One area where there is great variation between school practice is in relation to accessing and copying personal educational plans for children with special educational needs or disabilities (SEND).

Critical questions

» *What guidance have you already received at your training institution in relation to digital safeguarding protocols?*

» *In particular what do you know about:*

- *gaining permission to take digital photographs, how to pixelate identifying features, etc;*

- *accessing and storing pupil data?*

Generic guidance is often contained in course and placement handbooks. If you are unable to locate this information, it is a valid question to ask of your tutors.

- *Each time you visit a school ask what personal information about children you are permitted to have access to, whether you are allowed to copy that information and remove it from school premises, and if you are to photograph and record children.*

Acceptable Use Policies

The schools you visit will have a number of policies where e-safety may be highlighted, for example, behaviour, safeguarding and anti-bullying policies (Ofsted, 2014, p 8). As you read through the following sections it should become clear to you why e-safety has a specific mention in these contexts. One key document you should ensure you gain access to and fully understand when starting at a new school is the Acceptable Use Policy (AUP). Each school must have their own AUP that details how internet services are provided within that setting, details of filtered or managed systems, key information for parents and guidelines for use by staff and pupils. A partnership approach involving teachers, children, governors and parents is key to developing mutual understanding. A key issue is whether these policies are updated regularly to take account of new technologies and trends. Importantly AUPs should point out positive uses of technology rather than being simply a list of don'ts (Becta, 2009, p 31).

Becta outlined basic principles for an AUP including:

- *be clear and concise;*

- *reflect the setting;*

- *encourage end-user input;*

- *be written in a style and tone appropriate to the end-user;*

- *promote positive uses of new and emerging technologies;*

- *clearly outline acceptable and unacceptable behaviours when using technology and network resources provided by the school;*

- *clearly outline acceptable and unacceptable behaviours when using personal technologies on school premises or networks;*

- *clearly outline what network monitoring will take place;*

- *clearly outline the sanctions for unacceptable use;*

- *be regularly reviewed and updated;*

- *be widely, and regularly, communicated to all stakeholder groups.*

(Becta, 2009, pp 30–2)

Critical questions

Critically evaluate the AUP of a school you have visited. These are often available online via the school's website.

» *Are the responsibilities of all parties made clear?*

» *Are conduct expectations clear and are consequences for breach identified?*

» *When was it last updated?*

» *Are current trends in technology and application use reflected?*

» *If you have the opportunity ask children what their understanding and opinion is.*

During an inspection Ofsted may ask similar questions of pupils, for example: '*can you tell me one of the rules your school has for using the internet?*' or '*can you describe the risks of posting inappropriate content on the internet?*' (2014, p 13).

Identifying and understanding risk and potential dangers

Overview

This section of the chapter is designed to give you the basic information regarding risk necessary to meet your professional responsibilities; it is not exhaustive but will give you some insight into unfamiliar topics and a useful framework to organise your thinking. Sexual risk, cyberbullying and commercial risks are explored in some detail alongside an exploration of what is meant by a digital footprint and the positive and negative implications of this data trail.

In 2007 Dr Tanya Byron was commissioned by the UK government to undertake a comprehensive review on e-safety, in particular the internet and video games, and provide guidelines for industry and educational establishments amongst others. Byron *'approached classification of the online risks to children in terms of content, contact and conduct in line with a model developed by the EU Kids Online project'* originally by Hasebrink et al published in 2007 (2008, p 4). Many national bodies have since adopted this classification of risk, for example, Ofsted classifies e-safety as encompassing three areas of risk: content, contact and conduct (2014, p 4):

*   *content: being exposed to illegal, inappropriate or harmful material;*

*   *contact: being subjected to harmful online interaction with others;*

*   *conduct: personal online behaviour that increases the likelihood of, or causes harm.*

Table 9.1 *Opportunities and risks for children online*

		Condent: Child as recipient	Contact: Child as participant	Conduct: Child as actor
Opportunities	**Education learning and digital literacy**	Educational resources	Contact with others who share one's interests	Self-initiated or collaborative learning
	Participation and civic engagement	Global information	Exchange among interest groups	Concrete forms of civic engagement
	Creativity and self-expression	Diversity of resources	Being invited/inspired to create or participate	User-generated content creation
	Identity and social connection	Advice (personal/health/sexual etc)	Social networking, shared experiences with others	Expression of identity
Risks	**Commercial**	Advertising, spam, sponsorship	Tracking/harvesting personal information	Gambling, illegal downloads, hacking
	Aggressive	Violent/gruesome/hateful content	Being bullied, harassed or stalked	Bullying or harassing another
	Sexual	Pornographic/harmful sexual content	Meeting strangers, being groomed	Creating/uploading pornographic material
	Values	Racist, biased info/advice (eg, drugs)	Self-harm, unwelcome persuasion	Providing advice eg, suicide/pro-anorexia

Source: Livingstone, S., and Haddon, L. (2009) EU Kids Online: Final Report. LSE, London: EU Kids Online. Available at http://eprints.lse.ac.uk/24372/

The EU Kids Online model reproduced below provides a balanced overview of online risks and opportunities for children considering them in three possible roles: recipient, participant and actor. Considering these three roles encourages us to think beyond the child as the victim and consider how the child might be involved in, for example, cyberbullying. Encouragingly this multiple perspective is echoed in the terminology adopted in the new computing curriculum, ie children should be taught to be respectful and responsible users. Further, the risks identified were categorised as either commercial, aggressive, sexual or values by Livingston et al, giving a comprehensive matrix for thinking about e-safety.

Sexual risks

Sexual risks are often the dimension that reaches the headlines most frequently and can include:

- a child (recipient role) accessing, intentionally or unintentionally, materials which are pornographic or highly sexualised and not age appropriate;

- a child (participant role) having unwanted contact with strangers or known persons and being stalked or groomed. Grooming can be defined as *'a process by which a person prepares a child for abuse with the specific goal of gaining access to the child, their compliance and maintaining secrecy'* (Craven et al, 2006). The grooming process itself can take a variety of forms including *'bribery, gifts, flattery, threats, blackmail, sexualised games and desensitisation via exposure pornographic materials and/or child abuse images online or using a webcam'* (CEOP, 2014);

- a child (actor role) themselves creating, uploading and/or sharing inappropriate and/or sexual material including images online or via text known as *'sexting'* or SGII (self generated indecent image). In particular, it is vital to explore with children that once an image is shared digitally it cannot be recalled or deleted when an action is regretted. The image could be static or recorded by either party using a webcam. If the image is of a third party this in itself has legal implications and may be part of cyberbullying activities (see discussion below).

Cyberbullying

The risk of aggressive online behaviour can also prove very traumatic for children and young adults. Many professionals will have heard of the term of cyberbullying and how new technologies can mean that bullying can take place 24 hours a day, seven days a week beyond the school day. A range of platforms may be utilised including mobile phones, websites, forums, social media and networking, making it key that you know how these applications and tools work even if you are not a user in your own personal life. Without this detailed knowledge you will not be able to easily fulfil your professional responsibility to educate children about them.

A particularly troubling dimension with cyberbullying is that the perpetrator can fairly easily remain hidden or anonymous to the victim; sometimes imitating another person. Combined with the anonymity dimension the time and space dynamics can be far-reaching, traumatic and terrifying for the victim with little opportunity for escape or respite. Teachers have also been victims of cyberbullying and sensible precautions will be discussed in Chapter 10. Key to both children who are recipients of cyberbullying and those who are actors involved in the bullying, is education about what constitutes cyberbullying, preventative strategies, collecting evidence, reporting instances and potential consequences. Sometimes those initiating the cyberbullying may not think through the consequences of their actions initially and lack awareness of the devastating impact their actions may have on the recipient. Whilst bullying is not a new phenomenon, the scale and potential audience, alongside the disconnection from the physical world technology brings, means that as a trainee teacher you need to have an up-to-date awareness of the issue.

Beatbullying is an international charity seeking to support and educate about bullying, including cyberbullying, and defines it as '*when someone uses technology, like the internet or a mobile phone, to deliberately hurt, humiliate, harass, intimidate or threaten someone else*' (www.beatbullying.org). Further, cyberbullying can take many forms, including: '*unpleasant or threatening texts or emails, posting abusive messages online, posting humiliating or embarrassing videos or pictures online, spreading rumours, setting up or contributing to a hate site or group, imitating someone else and prank calling, texts or messages*' (www. beatbullying.org).

CASE STUDY

Cyberbullying dilemma

Whilst on placement, trainee Isla is approached by a Year 5 girl from her class at break time. The girl is upset as the previous evening she received a SMS text message on her mobile phone saying unkind things. The message did not say who it was from and she did not recognise the number. She has been worrying about who has sent it and whether it is someone she knows at school. She deleted the message but is worried there might be another one tonight.

Critical questions

» *Is this a case of cyberbullying?*

» *What criteria would you use to help you decide?*

» *What initial advice would you give the child?*

» *What follow-up actions would you take?*

The Thinkuknow Cybercafe resource at www.thinkuknow.co.uk/8_10/cybercafe/ Cyber-Cafe-Base/ contains a number of text message scenarios that may help you decide on your responses.

Commercial risks

Commercial risks to children are often overlooked but you need to be able to support children in understanding the possible risks and how to respond appropriately. The internet often requires age information when signing up on sites however the lack of viable checks often lead children to sign up as older than they actually are. Anybody with an email address is familiar with the volume of spam and unsolicited mail received. You need to provide children with some informed guidance about illegal downloading sites and the potential consequences. Copyright in relation to music and film in particular is an area where awareness-raising of ownership and intellectual property is needed. This topic was explored in Chapter 7. In relation to e-safety consider whether you are a good role model for the children you are working with.

Educating children to be critical of web-based information extends beyond everyday lessons and should cover whether material is biased, racist or prejudicial also. There is also a worrying occurrence of sites promoting self-harm or pro-anorexia for example. Whilst teenagers may be at the greatest risk some awareness amongst primary teachers seems sensible.

Digital footprints

Relevant to many of the potential dangers outlined in the previous section is helping children to understand that activity online leaves a digital footprint. From a positive perspective this provides an evidence trail when reporting abuse. On the negative side this means an individual loses ownership of a digital artefact, for example, a photo, when it is posted online as they cannot be certain another person has not saved a version.

An important strategy you need to educate children about is that a digital data trail exists that can be collated and shared with a responsible adult when reporting the problem. Children need to understand that whatever is said, posted, shared or written online leaves a digital footprint or trail that can be tracked. Once an image is published no one can be sure it has not been accessed and downloaded by another party. Many social networking profiles reveal information about a person's location, school attended, friends, hobbies, etc, and unless appropriate privacy settings are applied to restrict access, this information is essentially public. Educating parents about their own online profiles and what is revealed about their children is also important if you are involved in a parent education event (CEOP, 2014). A thought-provoking analogy from one of the CEOP videos features a young girl posting a photo and details about herself on an online profile and asking children to recognise that the real-world equivalent would be handing out a flyer of the same information to unknown members of the public. Your role as a teacher is to facilitate children understanding the real-world equivalent of some of their online behaviours. You also need to understand levels of risk that certain action or inaction may create and know how to effectively minimise risk without negating the many benefits involved with online social interaction.

Children's use of technology

Overview

This section gives an overview of research on the patterns of technology use by children of primary age and explores social networking, instant messaging and games consoles including communication functions.

Over time an increasing range of devices allow internet access, including laptops, tablet computers, smartphones, fixed and portable games consoles, televisions, PCs and other handheld devices. Previously many families may have relied upon children accessing the internet via the family computer located in a communal space; however, now these methods of access are greater, smaller, more portable and WiFi enabled. As a result a greater number of children may be accessing the internet more frequently and in private on devices that are personalised where they may be the sole user. These trends are likely to continue to grow. This presents problems for some adults, including parents and teachers, who may feel disconnected or less aware than the children they are responsible for. Ofcom in 2013 reported that only four in ten parents have parental controls installed at home and around half of parents perceive their child as knowing more about the internet than they do.

Some trainee and practising teachers reading this chapter will be in danger of thinking this discussion relates primarily to teenagers and only a small minority of older primary school children. However, data from Ofcom in 2013 suggest some surprising trends.

Children aged three to four years old:

* *28% use a tablet computer at home;*

* *12% of this age range use a tablet computer to go online;*

* *58% of this age range played games online at least weekly.*

Children aged eight to eleven years old:

* *18% owned a smartphone;*

* *18% owned a tablet computer;*

* *schoolwork/homework is the most commonly mentioned internet activity carried out at least weekly 75%, followed by games 54% and information 45%;*

* *making and receiving voice and video calls (Skype or Facetime) has increased to 10%;*

* *5% photo sharing websites such as Flickr, Instagram and Snapfish;*

* *about 22% have an active profile on a social networking site such as Facebook, Bebo or MySpace;*

* *83% of 8–11 year olds say they are confident about how to stay safe online;*

* *4% say they have experienced online bullying in the last year;*

* *17% say they use the internet mainly in their bedroom.*

(Ofcom, 2013, pp 4–9)

Social networking

Popular social networking sites including Facebook, Twitter and Instagram allow users to create a profile. A profile can contain a range of personal information including combinations of: name, age, address, contact details, email address, phone numbers, photographs, likes, dislikes, hobbies, links to or embedded photo albums or videos. When accessed via smart-phone devices the geo-location services, if enabled, can locate a user in time and space. Individuals can build up a friend list that typically contains a mix of people they know in the real world and those they only know in the virtual world. Usually only an email address is required to set up an account which makes it very easy to create false accounts. Friendship requests can be sent and received. What is particularly confusing to many children is the desire to be popular and amass a large friend list even if this involves people they do not know in the real world or have had limited contact with.

Key to using social networking sites in a safe way are privacy settings. By default these settings are often set on public when signing up and creating a profile. The user is actively required to change the settings themselves and may also need to do this for different functions within the site, for example, photo access and newsfeed updates, and to regularly check settings, as changes are fairly frequent on these platforms. Currently on Facebook privacy settings can be applied to who can access/see information about and updates posted and who can make contact. In relation to access settings, options include: public, friends, only me, close friend or family lists. Similarly basic or strict filtering can be applied to contact permissions alongside options such as everyone and friends of friends. A detailed understanding of the implications and nuances of each is important.

The concepts of *friends* and *to friend someone* have very unique and specific meanings in social networking terms and the implications need to be fully understood. Inviting someone, or accepting an invitation from a person, to add to a friend list means that individual will sub-sequently see everything on a profile, past and future, where the privacy setting has been set to *visible to friends*. Often children's friend lists contain a mixture of people they know in the real world and people they only know online. Another common privacy setting is *visible to friends of friends*, meaning that people not known to the owner can view their information and updates. This functionality could potentially mean a great deal of personal information could be harvested by an unknown person.

Facebook requires users to be 13, but other than entering an appropriate date of birth no other checks are in place. Facebook does have a Family Safety Centre at www.facebook.com/safety/ offering advice for parents and those working with children. Location based services on phones are often embedded in applications such as Facebook and locate an individual in time and space.

There are also social networking sites targeted at younger audiences, a popular example is Club Penguin (www.clubpenguin.com). Club Penguin offers children of all ages a range of games, activities and opportunities to chat with other users. The child uses a penguin avatar they can customise and earn coins by playing games. The site has some inbuilt safety fea-tures, including: live moderators and filtered chat, an ad-free environment and some parental tools. There are an estimated 300 million users of this Disney-owned site (CEOP, 2014, p 8).

Instant messaging

Instant messaging is about communicating in real time either within another application or using a specific tool. Instant messaging can allow file transfers including photographs and become web chat when a webcam is attached and activated. When a webcam is being used it is important to be aware that images can be recorded and later manipulated. When using instant messaging children should be reminded that: it is not advisable to swap files when you don't know who the other person is; to use a screen name that is gender neutral; be choosy about who to include on their list of contacts; not to give personal details; and use the safety features of their instant messaging software, eg block or ignore unwanted contacts.

Games consoles

Some teachers and parents may be unaware that popular games consoles connect to the internet, allow contacts to be built and both synchronous and asynchronous discussion to take place. Children who are at home in a safe and relaxed environment can feel protected, have a false sense of security and let their guard down. There are also well-being considerations for teachers to be aware of such as gaming addiction, overuse and children self-reporting long hours of game playing the evening before.

Reporting abuse and sources of support for children

Ofsted's inspection guidance on e-safety enquires about a school's ability to '*have appropriate mechanisms to intervene and support any incident*' (2014, p 4). Further, a key feature of good or outstanding practice specifies robust and integrated reporting routines where school-based reporting routes via designated staff are clearly understood and used by the whole school, and there is effective use of peer mentoring and support including clearly signposted channels (Ofsted, 2014, p 8) such as report abuse buttons (eg CEOP). Inadequate practice would include children not being aware of how to report a problem (p 9). Sample questions for children are also included:

- *If you felt uncomfortable about anything you saw, or if anyone asked you for your personal details such as your address on the internet would you know where to go for help?*

- *If anybody sent you hurtful messages on the internet or on your mobile phone would you know who to tell?*

                                                                    (Ofsted, 2014, p 13)

Critical question

A further question for staff and pupils directly relates to cyberbullying: 'are there clear reporting mechanisms with a set of actions in place for staff or pupils who feel they are being bullied online?' (Ofsted, 2014, p 14)

» *Consider how children in your class would respond to these sample questions.*

Child Exploitation and Online Protection Centre (CEOP) button

One well-established reporting mechanism is via the Child Exploitation and Online Protection Centre (CEOP) Report Abuse button.

The CEOP button enables children and young people, parents, carers and professionals to report any concerns they may have about potential grooming and suspicious child sex offender activity online. It provides a direct line to report to CEOP.

(CEOP, 2014, p 3)

Children under 11 are encouraged to report to a trusted adult who can help them complete the online information (CEOP, 2014, p 3). Once the button has been pressed you are taken to a page where navigation can be chosen according to age or parent/carer status. If immediate help is needed calling 999 is recommended. There are also other sources of support available, for example Childline and Cybermentors, offering children the opportunity to obtain advice from other children who have undergone specialist training. Advice screens are written in a child-friendly way offering both further sources of information or a further button to make an actual report where details of the incident or concern will need to be completed.

CEOP add-ons are available for all internet browsers to facilitate children only ever being one click away from being able to report concerns and CEOP has its own Facebook page, www.facebook.com/clickceop. Instructions for adding the CEOP button to a school website can be obtained through the Thinkuknow website following registration.

Handling disclosure

For a trainee the thought of a child making a disclosure can be a nerve-wracking time. Each school will have precise protocols in place including designated members of senior staff. You should always consult the school you are in for this information. The guidance included here is based on information provided in CEOP Ambassador training and is not meant to replace localised procedures but offer some generic common-sense advice in the event that your e-safety session brings forth an unexpected disclosure from a child.

Should a child make a disclosure directly to you:

- *keep calm;*
- *reassure the child;*
- *consider who else can hear;*
- *listen carefully;*
- *do not ask leading questions or promise confidentiality;*
- *inform the school's child protection officer (CPO) or deputy for safeguarding without delay;*
- *remember to record the child's words as accurately as possible as soon as you can. Time, date and sign the recording.*

(CEOP, 2014)

Critical points

Ofsted (2014) has a sample list of questions for all staff members that you as a trainee teacher need to be able to answer confidently and positively on each school placement.

» Have you had any training that shows the risks to your pupils' online safety?

» Are there policies in place that clearly demonstrate good and safe internet practice for staff and pupils?

» Are there sanctions in place to enforce the above policies?

» Do all staff understand what is meant by the term cyberbullying and the effect it can have on themselves and pupils?

» Are there clear reporting mechanisms with a set of actions in place for staff or pupils who feel they are being bullied online?

» Does the school have any plans for an event on Safer Internet Day? (This is an annual event, which has been going for some time, so schools that participate will know about the event.)

Further reading and useful resources

• Know IT All for Primary School Teachers '*is an award winning resource designed especially for primary school staff to help them understand important e-safety issues and how to get the most out of the internet*': www.childnet.com/resources/know-it-all-for-primary.

• '*CEOP's Thinkuknow programme provides a range of free educational resources – films, lesson plans, presentations, practitioner guidance, games and posters – to professionals working with children and young people*': www.thinkuknow.co.uk/.

• Cross et al reported that '*16% of children with a Statement of Special Educational Needs, while no more likely than their peers to be cyber-bullied overall, are significantly more likely to be targets of persistent cyber-bullying (harassment that is repeated and ongoing over a period of weeks or months to years)*' (2012, p 15). Targeted resources for use with children are available at KnowITAll for Teachers – SEN: www.childnet.com/resources/know-it-all-for-teachers-sen.

• The Beatbullying website also offers individualised support via the 'I need to talk' option with the options to access a cyber mentor for support, to send an urgent message to a counsellor or visit the support forum: www.beatbullying.org/about_this_site/what_is_cyberbullying/.

References

Beatbullying (2014) What is Cyberbullying? [online] Available at: www.beatbullying.org/about_this_site/what_is_cyberbullying/ (accessed 31 October 2014).

Becta (2009) *AUPs in Context: Establishing Safe and Responsible Online Behaviours.* [online] Available at: webarchive.nationalarchives.gov.uk/20101102103654/publications.becta.org.uk/display.cfm?resID=39286 (accessed 31 October 2014).

CEOP (Child Exploitation and Online Protection Centre) (2014) www.thinkuknow.co.uk/Teachers/Training/paidtrainingdetails/ (accessed 5 November 2014).

Child Exploitation and Online Protection Centre (2013) *Thinkuknow Introduction Script for Ambassadors*.

Craven, S, Brown, S and Gilchrist, E (2006) Sexual Grooming of Children: Review of Literature and Theoretical Considerations. *Journal of Sexual Aggression*, 12(3): 287–99.

Cross, E-J, Piggin, R, Douglas, T and Vonkaenal-Flatt, J (2012) *Virtual Violence II: Progress and Challenges in the Fight against Cyberbullying*. [online] Available at: www2.beatbullying.org/pdfs/Virtual-Violence-II.pdf (accessed 31 October 2014).

Department for Children, Schools and Families, and the Department for Culture, Media and Sport (2008) *Safer Children in a Digital World: The Report of the Byron Review*. [online] Available at: webarchive.nationalarchives.gov.uk/20101021152907/http://publications.education.gov.uk/eorderingdownload/dcsf-00334-2008.pdf (accessed 31 October 2014).

Department for Education (2011) *Teachers' Standards: Guidance for School Leaders, School Staff and Governing Bodies*. [online] Available at: www.gov.uk/government/uploads/system/uploads/attachment_data/file/208682/Teachers__Standards_2013.pdf (accessed 31 October 2014).

Department for Education (2013) *The National Curriculum in England: Framework Document*. [online] Available at: www.gov.uk/government/uploads/system/uploads/attachment_data/file/210969/NC_framework_document_-_FINAL.pdf (accessed 31 October 2014).

Hasebrink, U, Livingstone, S, Haddon, L, Kirwil, L and Ponte, C (2007) *EU Kids Go Online: Comparing Children's Online Activities and Risks across Europe*. LSE, London: EU Kids Online.

Livingstone, S and Haddon, L (2009) *EU Kids Online: Final Report*. London School of Economics. [online] Available at: www.lse.ac.uk/media@lse/research/EUKidsOnline/EU%20Kids%20I%20(2006-9)/EU%20Kids%20Online%20I%20Reports/EUKidsOnlineFinalReport.pdf (accessed 31 October 2014).

Office of Communications (2013) *Children and Parents: Media Use and Attitudes Report*. [online] Available at: stakeholders.ofcom.org.uk/binaries/research/media-literacy/october-2013/research07Oct2013.pdf (accessed 31 October 2014).

The Office for Standards in Education, Children's Services and Skills (2014) *Inspecting e-Safety in schools: Briefing for Section 5 Inspection*. Ref no: 120196.

10 Conclusion

Review

At the outset of this book you may have had a general understanding of the term digital literacy and some ideas on how it could impact on teaching and learning in your classroom. As you have journeyed through the book it is hoped that you now understand the need to think about digital literacies in plural, as there are wide-ranging facets. You have been prompted to consider your, and the children's, roles, as consumers or authors, working individually or collaboratively. The nature and scope of information today has been reflected upon and it has been acknowledged that today's learners face very different challenges and opportunities in learning with technology when compared to their teachers' school experiences.

Each chapter has made clear links to the computing national curriculum but emphasised a holistic cross-curricular approach. Table 10.1 provides an overview of where digital literacy aspects of the computing national curriculum have been covered.

Each chapter has also given an overview of how the topics under discussion relate to the Teachers' Standards. Table 10.2 gives an overview of where particular elements have been discussed. Please note that teaching and learning is a holistic activity so that a discrete link is not always possible but you will have been guided on how you could interpret the statements in relation to each topic.

You have been encouraged to avoid technological determinism and base implementation decisions on sound pedagogical reasoning. Chapter 2 explored in greater depth how your evolving digital literacy capability could enhance your teaching. Technologies were identified that might be useful in key professional roles, including: communicating subject knowledge, assessment, feedback, administration and extending learning beyond the boundaries of the classroom. Teaching and learning have a reciprocal relationship so Chapter 3 sought to highlight the contribution of digital literacy capability for learning. Analysis began by focusing on personalisation, ownership and autonomy.

Table 10.1 *Overview of computing national curriculum by chapter*

	Ch1	Ch2	Ch3	Ch4	Ch5	Ch6	Ch7	Ch8	Ch9
Computing POS	✓				✓				
Aims	✓								
Key Stage 1									
Understand what algorithms are …									
Create and debug …					✓				
Use logical reasoning to predict …									
Use technology purposefully to …	✓				✓				
Use technology safely and …	✓								✓
Recognise common uses …	✓								
Key Stage 2									
Design, write and debug programs …					✓				
Use sequence, selection and repetition in programs …									
Understand computer networks …	✓			✓			✓		
Use search technologies effectively …	✓			✓					
Use technology safely …	✓								✓
Select, use and combine …	✓	✓			✓				

Table 10.2 Overview of Teachers' Standards discussion by chapter

Teachers' Standards Part 1	Ch1	Ch2	Ch3	Ch4	Ch5	Ch6	Ch7	Ch8	Ch9
S1	1a		1b				1a		
S2	2b 2d	2d, e	2e		2d				
S3	3	3a		3a		3c			3a, b
S4	4d	4c, e	4b		4e				
S5		2							
S6		6				6			
S7			7c						
S8		8e							
Teachers' Standards Part 2								x	

You may have begun this book believing digital literacy was mainly about information literacy as this is a commonly identified area. Chapter 4 gave an overview of the information landscape, identifying the skills and understanding needed to effectively navigate the vast possibilities. The analysis extended beyond text to include audio and graphic information. The need for critical and evaluative skills could be argued to be greater for learners today than in previous generations.

Taking on the authoring role, Chapter 5 encouraged you to appreciate the vast number of choices available for creating digital content across modalities and suggested some primary appropriate tools to begin exploring. Throughout the book you have been encouraged to use technology with a purpose, to achieve authentic goals and share with an audience when appropriate.

Chapter 6 picked up the theme of communication, collaboration and sharing possibilities in a networked world. A detailed comparison and analysis of Web 2.0 tools took place, including: blogs, wikis and podcasting to assist you in your professional decisions about fitness for purpose.

With these rich opportunities come responsibilities as digital citizens. Chapter 7 explored the various dimensions of digital citizenship and included a practical focus on approaches to teaching these. Understanding traditional and new forms of copyright is crucial when you are repurposing and remixing content originally created by others for new purposes. The importance of data security was explored in relation to your professional duties.

Chapters 8 and 9 continued to develop the safeguarding theme from teachers' and learners' perspectives. As a teacher you were encouraged to take stock of your digital footprint and consider whether what your online presence conveyed was professional. Simple protocols were suggested for keeping your private and professional online profiles separate. Chapter 9 unpicked the risks and opportunities for learners in relation to e-safety and highlighted key school documentation that it is essential you become familiar with. An overview of reliable resources for this sensitive and vital topic were listed.

Where next?

One presentation at the 2014 BETT show by Handley was entitled *Let's get 'appy': why teachers should take note of apps* (Handley, 2014). We believe that tablet devices such as the iPad and the use of apps are bringing about a cultural step in terms of technology in education. Suddenly static tools of the past, expensive software, local storage and timetabled access are appearing very dated and restrictive. Teachers cannot afford to miss this shift and may need to radically rethink previous models of technology deployment.

Handley (2014) expands:

> *It's been nearly impossible to miss the surge of 'apps' – both on devices and web based over the past couple of years. Nearly everyone has a smartphone and/or tablet, and these devices have become increasingly common in schools over the past couple of years.*

> *There are also a large number of 'web apps' which can be accessed on practically any web-enabled device, including desktops and laptops, and therefore it is no surprise that an increasing number of teachers are starting to exploit the power of apps and that children are becoming more engaged by the use of apps.*

As with all technology, the tool/device/application itself is not *good* or *bad*, it is the purpose to which it is put that evokes a value judgement. From a positive perspective, apps are often very intuitive and easy to use compared to traditional list/menu programmes. They are often free or inexpensive. This is partly due to the volume and variety available and the simplicity of the creator to customer pathway with online app stores. App updates are regular, free and often automatic.

Handley goes further, suggesting that '*"apps" really come into their own when you exploit their potential to build home-school links and enable more meaningful work to be completed at home*' (2014).

Gardner and Davis (2014) caution about the '*pervasiveness of the app*' in allowing us to '*achieve a goal as expeditiously as possible*' (p 160).

> *At present life is certainly more than the sum of apps at our disposal. But the influence of apps is more pervasive and, we believe, potentially more pernicious.*

And that is because the breadth and the accessibility of apps inculcates an app consciousness, an app worldview: the idea that there are defined ways to achieve whatever we want to achieve, if we are fortunate enough to have the right ensemble of apps, and, at a more macroscopic level, access to the 'super app' for living a certain life, presented to the rest of the world in a certain way.

(Gardner and Davis, 2014, p 160)

We think this point further underlines the very purpose of this book: primary teachers and learners *need* to understand and engage with digital literacy to develop a critical stance that empowers them in their choices with technology. This can create the balance between being '*app-dependent versus app-enabled*' (Gardner and Davis, 2014).

This discussion of being *app-dependent versus app-enabled* resonates with Resnick's (2012) discussion of children going beyond being *consumers* to become *producers* of software and applications. A future edition of this book would include an extensive section on primary children creating apps, although currently this is very much in its infancy. Early adopters, like Handley (2014), are beginning to embrace this next step:

Finally, it is now even possible for children (and indeed teachers!) to easily create their own apps. There are an increasing number of services out there which allow you to create apps, which can be accessed as web apps on any mobile device, or (often for a fee) even published as 'real' apps to the different app stores. The children's favourite tool for allowing them to create their own apps is AppShed.

(www.appshed.com; www.bettshow.com/library/Let-s-get-appy-Why-teachers-should-take-note-of-apps#ixzz3CNTwu0e6)

Very much linked to this discussion are the growing number of 1:1 iPad/tablet projects. One-device-to-one-child projects are already beginning to make an impact in secondary schools. Spend a few moments exploring the case of Hove Park School at ipadteachers.org/year-groups/ks3/the-positive-impact-of-launching-a-1-1-ipad-project-the-data-from-hove-park-school/.

Some primary schools are beginning to explore the potential contribution to learning 1:1 ratio of handheld technology can make. We have included two brief examples for you to explore:

* Sciennes Primary – the 1:1 iPad classroom, digitallearningteam.org/2014/06/18/sciennes-primary-the-11-ipad-classroom/.

* St. Oliver Plunkett Primary School go 1:1 with the iPad, see www.academia.co.uk/case-study-st-oliver-plunkett-primary-school/.

Without doubt purchasing or leasing an iPad or similar tablet per child is expensive. One alternative is BYOD (Bring Your Own Device) initiatives and this approach has been explored in some further and higher education contexts. A balanced over of the pros and cons of implementing BYOD is given at www.teachthought.com/technology/12-pros-cons-to-byod/. In the short term we don't think this will impact greatly on primary provision.

On-going personal and professional development

For any educational professional keeping up to date with new technologies is challenging but the Teachers' Standards make it clear that there is a professional responsibility to keep up to date with subject knowledge as all primary teachers are responsible for delivering the computing programmes of study. Beyond this there is a responsibility to utilise approaches that are best suited to children's learning needs, approaches that are inclusive and creative, leading to the best outcomes for learners; this includes using digital tools. After many years in teacher education our stance is that you need to have a good understanding of the options to be able to make an informed decision. We are happy for any teacher to choose not to use technology when this decision is pedagogically based and not from lack of knowledge or an unwillingness to try something new. Critical and evaluative skills are equally as important as technological capability as sometimes your attempts at something new won't go as planned and you will need to be able to analyse why.

Whilst the previous statement is a bold one you need to be realistic: you will not become an expert at everything overnight. It takes time to learn prior to using tools with the children, time to plan and use new technologies in the classroom and time to reflect upon how it went. But this does not mean you shouldn't keep moving forward; you should consider it a journey and acknowledge that the end will constantly evolve and not be threatened by that. Learn something new each week and keep moving forward. It may well be the case that sometimes children in your class will know how to operate a tool better than you but be reassured that you remain the expert on the purpose of the task. You are modelling a learning journey yourself that children will readily relate to and no doubt enjoy showing you how to accomplish certain tasks. In discussion with a colleague a while back, who would not describe herself as tech-savvy, she articulated that *'if we held learners back to only doing the things we could do well it would be very boring for them'*. Be careful that you don't limit the scope of your learners' opportunities by defining them only in terms of your personal capability with technology.

Resources are undoubtedly an issue and there are competing demands on school funds. Rather than declare this as an insurmountable barrier and give up, take on the challenge – innovate, research and show that the technology you do have makes a difference in the classroom. The success of children using these tools is going to be more persuasive than anything else in persuading school leaders to invest further.

Chapter 9 explored the e-safety aspect of digital literacy. We would highly recommend further training with CEOP (Child Exploitation and Online Protection Centre): they offer courses designed for teachers.

*   There is an online course *Keeping Children Safe Online* (KCSO) designed to *'help you understand how children use the Internet and other digital technology. It's a joint initiative between the NSPCC and the NCA's CEOP command, aimed at any organisation or professional working with children'* (www.thinkuknow.co.uk/Teachers/KCSO/).

Face-to-face options include:

*   *thinkuknow Introduction course.* This free half-day training course is delivered by CEOP-trained Ambassadors (www.thinkuknow.co.uk/Teachers/Training/);

*   the CEOP Ambassador course (www.thinkuknow.co.uk/teachers/training/paidtrainingDetails/).

Overview of the CEOP Ambassador course

The Ambassador course is more in-depth than the Thinkuknow Introduction. It covers a wide range of areas, including:

*   *the nature of online offending against children;*

*   *how offenders use the online environment;*

*   *how young people use the internet and mobile technology;*

*   *risk taking behaviour of young people online, including digital footprints and sexting;*

*   *school and organisational responses and policy in this area*

On completion of the course, you will be able to download training materials which you can then use to train fellow professionals to deliver the Thinkuknow education programme to children and young people.

(CEOP, 2014)

There are several organisations we would suggest you join to assist you in keeping up to date in relation to digital literacy.

*   In terms of creative digital literacy and programming CAS (Computing at School) provide a wealth of resources to support classroom practice; professional articles and an online community – see www.computingatschool.org.uk.

*   Naace (National Association of Advisors for Computers in Education) *'is the national association for everyone promoting learning with technology in a connected world'* – see www.naace.co.uk.

*   ITTE (The Association for Information Technology and Teacher Education) is primarily an organisation for teacher educators, however, often there are excellent resources available on the website that can be utilised for continuing professional development; for example, an OER (open educational resource) series on Digital Literacy and Creativity – see www.itte.org.uk/node/816.

Each January the BETT show is held in London and offers opportunities for CPD, inspiration and shopping.

The BETT show (formerly known as the British Educational Training and Technology Show) is an annual trade show in the United Kingdom that showcases the use of information technology in education.

(en.wikipedia.org/wiki/BETT)

To find out about the next show and review highlights from previous shows see www.bettshow.com.

TED talks often challenge your thinking and there are a variety of talks about technology, social media, education, etc. at www.ted.com/topics/education. A useful informal advice and review site is Common Sense Media at www.commonsensemedia.org.

There are numerous blogs and wikis devoted to educational technology if you carry out an online search. Remember these are often articles of opinion and not research so you will still need to comprehensively explore whether they are appropriate for your circumstances. A few to try:

- Edudemic connecting education and technology at www.edudemic.com/best-education-technology/;

- Teachthought at www.teachthought.com/trends/30-trends-education-technology-2015/;

- Educational Origami at edorigami.wikispaces.com.

We hope the book has developed your understanding of digital literacy and inspired you to embrace some of the new tools in your teaching. Working in partnership with learners to explore digital tools will be an exciting opportunity.

We hope you have fun and your digital pedagogy continues to evolve and be invigorated by new developments.

References

CEOP (2014) www.thinkuknow.co.uk/Teachers/Training/paidtrainingdetails/ (accessed 5 November 2014).

Department for Education (2011) *Teachers' Standards: Guidance for School Leaders, School Staff and Governing Bodies*. [online] Available at: www.gov.uk/government/uploads/system/uploads/attachment_data/file/301107/Teachers__Standards.pdf (accessed 31 October 2014).

Department for Education (2013) *The National Curriculum in England: Framework Document*. [online] Available at: www.gov.uk/government/uploads/system/uploads/attachment_data/file/210969/NC_framework_document_-_FINAL.pdf (accessed 31 October 2014).

Gardner, H and Davis, K (2014) *The App Generation: How Today's Youth Navigate Identity, Intimacy, and Imagination in a Digital World*. London: Yale University Press.

Handley, T (2014) *Let's Get 'Appy': Why Teachers Should Take Note of Apps*. [online] Available at: www.bettshow.com/library/Let-s-get-appy-Why-teachers-should-take-note-of-apps (accessed 31 October 2014).

Hove Park School (2014) ipadteachers.org/year-groups/ks3/the-positive-impact-of-launching-a-1-1-ipad-project-the-data-from-hove-park-school/ (accessed 31 October 2014).

Resnick, M (2012) Reviving Papert's Dream. *Educational Technology*, 52(4): 42–6. [online] Available at: web.media.mit.edu/~mres/papers/educational-technology-2012.pdf (accessed 31 October 2014).

Sciennes Primary (2014) The 1:1iPad Classroom. [online] Available at: digitallearningteam. org/2014/06/18/sciennes-primary-the-11-ipad-classroom/ (accessed 31 October 2014).

St. Oliver Plunkett Primary School (2014) Go 1:1 with the iPad. [online] Available at: www.academia. co.uk/case-study-st-oliver-plunkett-primary-school/ (accessed 31 October 2014).

Wikipedia (2014) The BETT Show. [online] Available at: en.wikipedia.org/wiki/BETT (accessed 31 October 2014).

Index

Acceptable Use Policy (AUP), 115, 121, 137–8
adaptive memory effect, 44
advertising, digital commerce, 110
affordances, 28–9, 45
animation approaches, 81
attachments, 57
audio, creative tools, 82–3
audio file formats, 59
augmentation, 31
AUP, see Acceptable Use Policy

Barber, D, 102
beatbullying, 141
Beatwave, 83
Belshaw model of digital literacy, 11–14
Benjes-Small, C, 66
BIEC, see British Institute of Eating Control
bitmap, 57, 58
blogs/blogging
    case study, 91–2
    description, 91
    primary school, 92–3
    writing forms, 83–4
brain plasticity concept, 25
British Institute of Eating Control (BIEC), 109
Byron, T, 42, 139

Carr, N, 44
Carrington, V, 95, 96
Centre for Learning and Performance Technologies
        (CLPT), 31
CEOP, see Child Exploitation and Online Protection Centre
Child Exploitation and Online Protection Centre
        (CEOP), 145
citizenship, 106
civic component, 14
CLPT, see Centre for Learning and Performance
        Technologies
CMA, see Computer Misuse Act
Cogill, J, 27
cognitive components, 12
collaborative authoring, 94
collaborative learning, 94
comics, 86
commercial risks, 141

communicative component, 13
Computer Misuse Act (CMA), 112
computing national curriculum, 150
concept mapping, 79
confident component, 13
conjecture, 30
Conole, G, 29
constructive component, 13
content creation
    national curriculum and, 72–3
    Teachers' Standards and, 73
Cooper, L, 102
copyright, 113–14
Copyright Designs and Patents Act, 113
Creative Commons Licencing, 74
creative component, 14
creative tools
    audio, 82–3
    concept mapping, 79
    description, 76–7
    education, 76
    moving images, 80–2
    programming, 87
    social bookmarking, 77–8
    static images, 79–80
    writing forms, 83–6
creativity
    definitions, 73–4
    digital taxonomy, 76
    multimodality, 74
critical component, 14
Cuban, L, 29
cultural component, 11
curriculum development, 108
curriculum subject knowledge, 26
cyberbullying
    e-safety, 140–1
    teachers as targets, 128–9
cyberlearning modality, 49

data protection, 112
Data Protection Act (DPA), 112
data security, 112–13
databases, 55–7
Davis, K, 152

Day, D, 28
Department for Children Schools and Families
    (DfCSF), 128–9
descriptive modality, 43
Devine, J, 60
DfCSF, *see* Department for Children Schools and Families
digital citizens, 106
digital citizenship
    concept of, 106
    copyright, 113–14
    curriculum development, 108
    data protection, 112
    data security, 112–13
    definition, 107
    digital access, 114–16
    digital commerce, 110
    digital literacy, 109
    digital world, 106–7
    netiquette, 110–12
digital commerce, 110
digital footprints
    description, 121–2
    e-safety, 142
    geo-location services, 126
    online content, 122
    privacy settings, 125–6
    social networking, 123–5
digital immigrants, 25
digital literacy
    Belshaw model, 11–14
    challenges, 7–10
    components, 11–14, 17
    consumer/author, 9
    developmental process, 10
    digital citizenship, 109
    elements model, 12
    Hobbs model, 10, 18
    JISC definition, 9
    JISC model, 11
    national curriculum, 16–18
    nature and scope of information, 8
    organisations, 155–6
    Payton and Hague model, 14
    resources, 21–2
    single/plural, 9
    Teachers' Standards, 19–20
digital natives, 25
digital safeguarding, 137
digital taxonomy of creativity, 76
digital taxonomy of knowledge, 31
digital technology
    affordances, 28–9
    long-term memory, 43–7
    models of pedagogy, 26–8
    motivation, 48–50
    short-term memory, 42–3
digital technology tools
    categorisation, 31
    focus, 30

mode, 30–1
    pedagogy, 29
    quantity, 29–30
DPA, *see* Data Protection Act
Dweck, C, 48
Dyke, M, 29

e-books, 85–6
education
    creative tools for, 76
    social networking, 125
    value of podcasting, 100
    value of wiki, 95
Egger-Sider, F, 60
e-safety
    Acceptable Use Policies, 137–8
    commercial risks, 141
    cyberbullying, 140–1
    digital footprints, 142
    digital safeguarding, 137
    identifying risks, 139–40
    Internet provision in school, 134–5
    national curriculum requirements, 136–7
    sexual risks, 140
    Teachers' Standards, 135–6
Eynon, R, 25

Facebook, 123–4, 144
Facer, K, 7, 18
field types, 55
figurative modality, 43
file formats
    audio, 59
    GIF images, 58
    jpg/jpeg images, 57
    vector images, 58
    video, 59–60
Fitzgerald, A, 47
focus, 30
Fogarty, I, 33

games consoles, 145
Gardener, H, 152
general pedagogical knowledge, 26
Georgsen, M, 19
Gibson, J J, 25
GIF images, 58
Google, 64
graphics file formats
    GIF images, 58
    jpg/jpeg images, 57
    vector images, 58
graphics software, 60
Green, H, 41

Hague model of digital literacy, 14
handling disclosure, 146
Harris, R, 66
Helsper, W J, 25

Hennessy, S, 33
Heppell, S, 106, 115
Hobbs digital literacy model, 10
horizontal search engines, 63
Housand, A, 50
Housand, B, 50
hyper-local blogs, 91

ICT, see Information and Communication Technology
ILS, see integrated learning system
Information Age, 106
Information and Communication Technology (ICT), 30
instant messaging, 144
integrated learning system (ILS), 35
interactive whiteboard (IW), 27, 32–3
IW, see Interactive Whiteboard

JISC, see Joint Information Systems Committee
Joint Information Systems Committee (JISC), 9, 11
jpg/jpeg images, 57, 58

Kaye, L, 31
Kennewell, S, 28
KidBlog, 84
Kirklees Learning Service, 115, 116
Koehler, M, 27

Leander, K, 98, 99
learning modalities, 49
Lepper, M, 48
literacy multimodality, 46
Lloyd, M, 28
long-term memory
    adaptive memory effect, 44
    affordances, 45
    description, 43
    literacy multimodality, 46
    primary science multimodality, 46–7
    spacing effect, 44
    testing effect, 44
lossy, 57, 59
Loveless, A, 30

Malone, T, 48
Marzano, R, 32
Mayer, R, 42, 43
Mercer, N, 33
Merzenich, M, 25
microblogging, 125
Miller, M, 44
Mishra, P, 27
Miyake, N., 94
modality principle, 43
mode, 30–1
models of pedagogy, 26–8
modification concept, 31
Moreno, R, 42, 43
Mossberger, K., 106
motivation, 48–50

moving images
    approaches to animation, 81
    description, 80
    screencasting, 82
    stop frame animation, 81
    video editing, 81
multimedia, 43
multimodal creativity, 74
multimodal learning
    Cisco report on, 45
    literacy, 46
    primary science, 46–7
    short-term memory, 43

national curriculum
    computing, 150
    content creation, 72–3
    digital literacy, 16–18
    e-safety, 136–7
National Health Service (NHS), 55
negative behavior, 128–9
netiquette, 110–12
NHS, see National Health Service

object-based drawing, 80
Ofsted, 134, 139, 145
Ohler, J, 115
Otta, M, 50

painting. 80
Papert, S, 30, 41
Payton model of digital literacy, 14
pedagogical content knowledge, 26
pedagogy models, 26–8
photo editing, 79
pixel, 57
podcasting
    description, 99–100
    educational value of, 100
    getting started with, 100–1
    producing, 101
Prensky, M, 25, 99
primary school blogs, 92–3
professional conduct
    school policies, 121
    Teachers' Standards, 120–1
programming, 87
Puentedura, R, 31

quantity, 29–30

redefinition concept, 31
reporting abuse for children, 145–6
Resnick, M, 86
Richardson, W, 66, 91, 95
risks
    commercial, 141
    sexual, 140
Ryberg, T, 19

Scratch tool, 86
screencasting, 82
search engines
    description, 60
    Google, 64
    semantic, 62–3
    subject directories, 61
    vertical, 63
    visual, 61–2
search strategies
    operators, 65
    purpose, 64
    tactics, 65
    terms, 64
Selinger, M, 31
Selwyn, N, 33
semantic search engines, 62–3
sexual risks, 140
Shaffer, G, 92
short-term memory
    description, 42
    modality principle, 43
    multimodal learning, 43
    split-attention, 42
Shulman's model of pedagogy, 26
social bookmarking, 77–8
social networking
    education, 125
    Facebook, 123–4
    prevalence of, 123
    technology use by children, 143–4
spacing effect, 44
split-attention, 42
spreadsheets, 55–7
static images
    description, 79
    object-based drawing, 80
    painting, 80
    photo editing, 79
stop frame animation, 81
subject directories, 61
subject knowledge, 26
substitution, 31

Tapscot, D, 107
Tavella, M, 50
teacher knowledge, Shulman's perspectives, 26
teacher's digital identity
    cyberbullying, 128–9
    personal equipment in school, 127
    research projects and training assignments, 130–1
    school equipment, 126–7
teacher's tools
    assessment, 35–6
    extending learning beyond classroom, 33–5
    interactive whiteboard (IW), 32–3
Teachers' Standards
    content creation, 73
    discussion by chapter, 151

professional conduct, 120–1
technological content knowledge, 27
technological pedagogical content knowledge
    (TPCK), 27
technological pedagogical knowledge, 27
technology use by children
    games consoles, 145
    instant messaging, 144
    overview of, 142–3
    social networking, 143–4
testing effect, 44
Time magazine, 45
TPCK, *see* technological pedagogical content
    knowledge
Tremayne, M, 91
Twitter, 125

UK Copyright Service (UKCS), 113
UKCS, *see* UK Copyright Service

vector images, 58
vertical search engines, 63
vidcasts, 99
video editing, 81
video file formats, 59–60
virtual learning environments (VLEs), 34, 129–30
virtual world, 98–9
visual search engines, 61–2
VLEs, *see* virtual learning environments

Warwick, P, 33
Watkins, C, 94
web 2.0 blogging, 91
web 2.0 tools, 102
web logs, 91
web-based data
    content evaluation, 66
    search engines, 60–4
    search strategies, 64–5
    website evaluation, 66–7
websites, 66–7, 86
West, J, 94, 95, 96
West, M, 94, 95, 96
wiki
    apps, 97
    collaborative learning, 94
    description, 93
    educational value, 95
    entering, 94–5
    software, 97
    types of, 95–7
    writing forms, 84–5
writing forms
    blogging, 83–4
    comics, 86
    description, 83
    e-books, 85–6
    websites, 86
    wikis, 84–5